MILDREDS

VEGAN

COOKBOOK

MILDREDS

VEGAN

COOKBOOK

BRIGHT FOOD, BOLD FLAVOUR

RECIPES CREATED BY DANIEL ACEVEDO
& SARAH WASSERMAN

An Hachette UK Company
www.hachette.co.uk

First published in Great Britain in 2018 by Mitchell Beazley,
a division of Octopus Publishing Group Ltd, Carmelite House,
50 Victoria Embankment, London EC4Y 0DZ
www.octopusbooks.co.uk
www.octopusbooksusa.com

Design & layout copyright © Octopus Publishing Group Ltd 2018
Text copyright © Mildreds Limited 2018

Distributed in the US by Hachette Book Group, 1290 Avenue of the Americas,
4th and 5th Floors, New York, NY 10104

Distributed in Canada by Canadian Manda Group, 664 Annette St., Toronto,
Ontario, Canada M6S 2C8

ISBN 978-1-78472-373-6

A CIP catalogue record for this book is available from the British Library.

Printed and bound in China.

10 9 8 7 6 5 4 3 2 1

Publisher's note
Please note that liquid measurements in this book are given in imperial fluid
ounces and pints rather than US fluid ounces and pints.

Commissioning Editors: Eleanor Maxfield & Sarah Reece
Art Director: Yasia Williams-Leedham
Senior Editor: Leanne Bryan
Copy Editor: Jo Richardson
Designer: Grade Design
Photographer: Matt Russell
Home Economists: Aya Nishimura & Rosie Reynolds
Prop Stylist: Alexander Breeze
Production Manager: Caroline Alberti

CONTENTS

INTRODUCTION

Back in the late 1980s, when London's Soho was still edgy, we launched Mildreds on an unsuspecting public. Those were the days when diners were all too accustomed to vegetarian food being brown and 'worthy', dished up on earthenware pottery. But our aim at Mildreds was - and still very much is - to deliver an inspiring eating experience with fresh, vibrant vegetarian dishes featuring ideas from a wide variety of culinary styles.

Despite prophecies of early closure from the local community, which gave us six months at the most, Mildreds thrived from the start and has gone from strength to strength to become the world-renowned restaurant it is today. The original Soho restaurant has now been joined by three sister restaurants in Camden, Kings Cross and Dalston, and in 2015 *Mildreds The Cookbook* was published, showcasing some of our favourite recipes from the restaurant.

We are now extremely proud to present *Mildreds Vegan Cookbook*, where we have chosen to focus exclusively on vegan cooking. Although Mildreds is a vegetarian restaurant, many of our dishes are vegan and these are some of the most popular choices on our menu. With mounting pressure to reduce greenhouse gasses, increase sustainability and bring an end to intensive farming, as well as the need to gain more knowledge and assume greater responsibility over what we choose to cook and eat, a global vegan movement is slowly but surely edging its way centre stage.

Executive chef Daniel Acevedo and development chef Sarah Wasserman have again collaborated to create a book full of exciting recipes that, as always, seek to dispel any misconceptions that may still be associated with vegan food. Inspired by cuisines from around the world, and constantly exploring new ideas and experimenting with flavours and techniques, they have compiled a collection that offers a riot of taste, colour and texture to delight any palate.

Jane Muir, founder of Mildreds

As well as plenty of dishes for everyday meals, Daniel and Sarah show that social gatherings with a vegan spread can be indulgent, delicious and satisfying - generous both in proportions and flavour. Whether it's for a brunch with friends, a summer barbecue, a celebration dinner or a children's party, there are dishes to wow everyone, from delectable savoury-filled pastries and dumplings and crowd-pleasing Turkish-style pizzas to fun-coloured (the natural way) party cakes and I can't-believe-they're-vegan desserts. These are all mouthwatering recipes that just happen to be vegan.

Vegan cooking is often regarded as a relatively complicated way of preparing food, and it can seem daunting to make the move away from the more traditional approach to working with unfamiliar ingredients. But there is now an abundance of vegan ingredients and substitutes readily available at all major supermarkets, and we show you how a well-stocked larder and refrigerator, together with a little forethought, can help make the process easier. There is, in any case, a good deal of pleasure and satisfaction to be had from planning your meals and spending a bit of extra time in their preparation to achieve the best results. And for those who want to be more adventurous, there is the opportunity here to make your own vegan cheese, cashew nut cream and "aquafaba" meringues along with dairy-free whipped cream. Daniel and Sarah have also included all the practical tips you need so that the techniques involved are as failsafe as possible.

You'll also find stamps at the top of many of the recipes to flag dishes that are gluten-free. Of course, other recipes can also be amended to suit your particular diet. For example, gluten-free flour can be substituted for regular flour in most instances.

The beautifully photographed recipes in *Mildreds Vegan Cookbook* demonstrate perfectly that a vegan diet the Mildreds way, whether followed full time or from time to time, will bring surprise, joy and colour to your life, and ensure your taste buds are well and truly alive and kicking!

**Executive chef
Daniel Acevedo and
development chef
Sarah Wasserman**

BRUNCH

GOLDEN & GOJI BERRY, FIG & COCONUT BIRCHER MUESLI

A simple and filling, healthy breakfast. Traditionally, Bircher muesli is made with dairy milk, cream or yogurt, but this coconut yogurt version has a lovely fresh finish instead and the berries add a tropical twist. Golden berry is another name for the physalis fruit, originating from South America – a small, round, golden fruit similar in size and flavour to a gooseberry, and also known as Cape gooseberry. Dried golden berries can be sourced from any good health store or online. You can switch up the fruit to any you prefer – dried mango or papaya would also work well. Use gluten-free oats to make this gluten-free.

1   Mix the oats, berries and figs with the yogurt and coconut milk in a bowl so that the mixture forms a thick whipped cream consistency. Cover with clingfilm and leave in the refrigerator preferably overnight or for at least 4-5 hours.

2   Before serving, add the orange juice to the bircher and mix through. If it looks too thick, add a splash more milk.

3   Serve topped with the apple batons, slices of banana and a drizzle of maple syrup. If you have them, a few toasted coconut flakes look and taste lovely too.

SERVES 2

100g (3½oz) good-quality porridge oats

25g (1oz) golden berries, chopped

25g (1oz) goji berries

4 dried figs, chopped

240ml (8½fl oz) coconut yogurt (or soya yogurt)

100ml (3½fl oz) light or full-fat coconut milk from a carton (not a can)

juice of 1 orange

TO SERVE

1 dessert apple, cut into batons

slices of banana

maple syrup

toasted coconut flakes (optional)

APPLE, CRANBERRY & APRICOT GRANOLA

A great breakfast staple, granola also makes a popular energy-filled snack. What's more, it's really simple to knock up at home, certainly easy enough to make with children. Homemade granola packed into an attractive jar or bag makes a nice gift too.

You can use any fruit or nuts you prefer or indeed dispense with them entirely if they're not your cup of tea. Having said that, if you do omit the nuts, be sure to replace them with an equal quantity of oats or the mixture will be too sticky. Equally, the maple syrup can be swapped for any other syrup, such as agave, though this will affect the flavour.

The apple and pecans give this granola a distinctly autumnal feel. Choose a red-skinned apple like a Katy or Red Pippin to get lovely little red threads running through the granola. Use gluten-free oats to make this gluten-free.

1   Preheat the oven to 170°C (340°F), Gas Mark 3½. Line 2 large baking sheets with baking parchment.
2   Combine the oats, nuts, seeds, grated apple, salt and spices in a large bowl.
3   Put the coconut oil, maple syrup and sugar in a small saucepan and heat gently, stirring, until the coconut oil is melted and the ingredients are combined.
4   Add the warm mixture to the ingredients in the bowl and mix thoroughly with a wooden spoon or rubber spatula.
5   Spread the mixture on to the lined baking sheets. Don't worry if there are lumps, but make sure the mixture is only a single layer deep.
6   Bake for 45 minutes–1 hour, stirring every 15 minutes or so, until the nuts are starting to colour. Don't worry if the granola still seems soft – it will firm up as it cools.
7   Remove from the oven and leave to cool slightly on the sheets. Then return the granola to the bowl and mix in the dried fruit.
8   Leave to cool completely, then store in a clean airtight container or jar for up to 3 weeks.

SERVES 6–8

200g (7oz) oats (we like jumbo, but any oats will work)
60g (2¼oz) flaked almonds
60g (2¼oz) pecan nuts
60g (2¼oz) pumpkin seeds
60g (2¼oz) grated dessert apple (grate on the large-holed side of a box grater)
¼ teaspoon sea salt flakes
pinch of grated nutmeg
¼ teaspoon ground cinnamon
75g (2¾oz) coconut oil
100ml (3½fl oz) maple syrup
30g (1oz) demerara sugar
75g (2¾oz) ready-to-eat dried apricots, roughly chopped
50g (1¾oz) dried cranberries

DARK CHOCOLATE, CHERRY & COCONUT GRANOLA

SERVES 6-8

200g (7oz) oats (we like jumbo, but any oats will work)

100g (3½oz) flaked almonds

80g (3oz) pecan nuts

¼ teaspoon sea salt flakes

pinch of grated nutmeg

¼ teaspoon ground cinnamon

75g (2¾oz) coconut oil

100ml (3½fl oz) maple syrup

30g (1oz) demerara sugar

3 tablespoons vegan cocoa powder

50g (1¾oz) coconut flakes

80g (3oz) vegan dark chocolate chips or dark chocolate bar chopped into small pieces (minimum 70% cocoa solids)

100g (3½oz) dried cherries

TO SERVE (OPTIONAL)

vegan crème fraîche or yogurt

Berry Compote (see page 18)

We serve this granola with Berry Compote (see page 18), made with raspberries, and coconut yogurt for breakfast - see the photograph overleaf. It's more like a treat than a super-healthy brekkie, so we also keep some around as a snack at home. Equally, you can use this as a yummy crunchy topping on vegan ice cream. If you can't find coconut flakes, you can use desiccated coconut, but the flakes do look amazing. Use gluten-free oats to make this gluten-free.

1   Preheat the oven to 170°C (340°F), Gas Mark 3½. Line 2 large baking sheets with baking parchment.

2   Combine the oats, nuts, salt and spices in a large bowl.

3   Put the coconut oil, maple syrup, sugar and cocoa powder in a small saucepan and heat gently, stirring, until the coconut oil is melted and the ingredients are combined.

4   Add the warm mixture to the ingredients in the bowl and mix thoroughly with a wooden spoon or rubber spatula.

5   Spread the coconut flakes out on one of the lined baking sheets and toast in the oven for 4-5 minutes, checking regularly as they burn easily, until the edges are golden. Remove from the oven and set the toasted coconut aside.

6   Spread the oat mixture on to both lined baking sheets. Don't worry if there are lumps, but make sure the mixture is only a single layer deep.

7   Bake for 45 minutes-1 hour, stirring every 15 minutes or so, until the nuts are starting to colour. Don't worry if the granola still seems soft - it will firm up as it cools.

8   Remove from the oven, add the chocolate and stir through so that it melts into the granola. Leave to cool slightly on the sheets. Then return the granola to the bowl and mix in the dried cherries and toasted coconut.

9   Leave to cool completely, then store in an airtight container or jar for up to 3 weeks. Serve with vegan crème fraîche or yogurt and berry compote, if liked.

BERRY COMPOTE

Berry compote (*see* photograph on previous page) is a brunch staple, excellent served with either pancakes or waffles (*see* opposite), or with our Dark Chocolate, Cherry and Coconut Granola (*see* page 15). Here are two versions: one raw, one cooked. You can use the recipes to make either a single berry compote, such as raspberry or blueberry, or a seasonal mix.

NO-COOK BERRY COMPOTE

1   Blend half the berries with the remaining ingredients in a blender.
2   Strain the mixture through a sieve to remove the seeds.
3   Combine with the remaining berries.

COOKED BERRY COMPOTE

This cooked version will give you a stronger-coloured compote and one that will keep for longer - store in the refrigerator, covered, for up to 3-4 days.

1   Put half the berries with the remaining ingredients in a saucepan and bring up to a simmer. Cook gently for 10-15 minutes, stirring frequently, until the berries have totally broken down and the liquid is glossy.
2   Take the pan off the heat and leave the compote to cool a little and then blend with a stick blender.
3   Strain the mixture through a fine-mesh sieve to remove the seeds, then mix with the remaining berries.

SERVES 4

NO-COOK BERRY COMPOTE
260g (9¼oz) berries (about 2 punnets)
50ml (2fl oz) agave syrup (or other syrup)
75ml (5 tablespoons) water
pinch of vanilla powder (optional)

COOKED BERRY COMPOTE
260g (9¼oz) berries (about 2 punnets)
100ml (3½fl oz) water
pinch of vanilla powder
squeeze of lemon juice
60g (2¼oz) caster sugar

PORRIDGE WAFFLES
WITH BRAMLEY APPLE SAUCE

MAKES 5-6 WAFFLES

200g (7oz) plain flour

50g (1¾oz) porridge oats

1 tablespoon baking powder

2 tablespoons caster sugar

½ teaspoon ground cinnamon

large pinch of salt

350ml (12fl oz) soya milk

2 tablespoons maple syrup

3 tablespoons light oil (such
  as groundnut or sunflower),
  plus extra for oiling

FOR THE APPLE SAUCE

450g (1lb) peeled and cored
  Bramley apples, cut into
  2-3cm (¾-1¼-inch) chunks

125g (4½oz) caster sugar

small knob of vegan margarine

¼ teaspoon ground cinnamon

splash of water

TO SERVE

maple syrup (or other syrup)

vegan crème fraîche or yogurt

handful of raspberries

As the saying goes, 'If you love someone, make them pancakes, but if you really love them, make them waffles.' With that in mind, this recipe will also work as pancakes if you don't have a waffle iron. The oats in these waffles make them really satisfying and crunchy, perfectly offset by the soft Bramley apple sauce. However, if you don't have time to make the apple sauce, serve with fresh berries. We top these off with maple syrup and a scattering of raspberries for the ultimate breakfast feast (see photograph on pages 16-17), and if you feel like throwing caution to the wind, you could serve them with vegan ice cream instead of the crème fraîche or yogurt.

1   For the apple sauce, place all the ingredients in a medium saucepan and cook gently for about 10-15 minutes until the apples have broken down, but it's OK if a few small chunks remain.

2   Measure out all the dry ingredients into a bowl and stir with a balloon whisk.

3   Measure out all the wet ingredients into a separate bowl and mix with the whisk.

4   Make a well in the centre of the dry mixture and add the wet mixture, then mix with the whisk just enough to bring together.

5   Heat the waffle iron to high and then lightly brush with oil.

6   Pour in the waffle mixture and close the iron. They will take 4-5 minutes to cook. You can keep the cooked waffles warm in a preheated oven while you finish cooking the whole batch or just put the waffle iron on the table and eat as you go.

7   Serve with the apple sauce (warm or cool, as you prefer), maple syrup, vegan crème fraîche or yogurt and a handful of raspberries.

WALNUT, DATE & CINNAMON ROLLS

There's nothing better to wake up to than the smell of cinnamon rolls and coffee (see photograph on pages 16-17). These can be prepared the day before and then baked in the morning.

1   Warm the milk, sugar and vegan margarine in a small saucepan, stirring to combine, and then pour into a bowl. Leave to cool until just above room temperature (35°C/95°F) and then stir in the yeast. Cover with clingfilm and leave to activate somewhere fairly warm for about 15 minutes until beginning to froth.

2   In a separate bowl, rub the flour and suet between your fingers until the suet is incorporated and the mixture is crumbly. Stir in the cardamom and salt. Add half the flour mixture to the bowl of milk and yeast and whisk together, then mix in the rest of the flour.

3   Oil a work surface, then turn the dough out and knead for 5-8 minutes until smooth. Return to the bowl, cover with clingfilm and leave to rise in a warm place for 35-40 minutes until doubled in size.

4   Meanwhile, for the filling, chop the dates and leave to soak in the warm orange juice, covered, in a warm place for at least 20 minutes.

5   Preheat the oven to 200°C (400°F), Gas Mark 6. Line a 25cm (10-inch) round springform tin with baking parchment.

6   Combine all the filling ingredients, except the dates and walnuts, in a small saucepan. Warm the mixture slightly so that the margarine starts to melt, making it easy to brush on to the dough.

7   Turn the dough out on to a floured work surface and roll out to a rectangle measuring 20 × 80cm (8 × 32 inches) and just shy of 5mm (¼ inch) thick. Brush with the sugar and cinnamon mixture. Drain any excess juice from the dates, then sprinkle them evenly over the dough along with the walnuts. Roll the dough into a log and slice into about 10 rolls, 8-10cm (3¼-4 inches) thick.

8   Lay the rolls flat in the lined tin so that the swirls are facing upwards - it's OK if they are touching. Cover with clingfilm and leave to rest at room temperature for 20 minutes. If you're making them the night before, pop them in the refrigerator at this point.

9   Brush the rolls with melted margarine and bake for 20-25 minutes until risen and golden brown. To glaze the rolls, brush them with maple syrup 5 minutes before the end of the baking. Transfer them to a wire rack to cool slightly before serving warm. These are best eaten fresh but will keep in an airtight container for up to 2 days.

MAKES ABOUT 10 ROLLS

300ml (10fl oz) almond milk (or other plant-based milk)

70g (2½oz) caster sugar

30g (1oz) vegan margarine, plus extra, melted, for brushing

7g (⅓oz) sachet fast-action dried yeast

500g (1lb 2oz) strong white flour, plus extra for dusting

70g (2½oz) vegetarian suet

seeds from 4 green cardamon pods, crushed with a pestle and mortar, or ½ teaspoon ground cardamom

pinch of salt

light oil (such as groundnut or sunflower), for oiling

maple syrup, for glazing (optional)

FOR THE FILLING

90g (3¼oz) pitted dried dates

50ml (2fl oz) warm orange juice

100g (3½oz) demerara sugar

1 tablespoon ground cinnamon

pinch of sea salt flakes

seeds from 1 vanilla pod

50g (1¾oz) vegan margarine

70g (2½oz) walnut pieces

CHOCOLATE, CARDAMOM & ALMOND ROLLS

MAKES ABOUT 10 ROLLS

300ml (10fl oz) almond milk
(or other plant-based milk),
plus extra for brushing

70g (2½oz) caster sugar

30g (1oz) vegan margarine

7g (⅓oz) sachet fast-action
dried yeast

500g (1lb 2 oz) strong white
flour, plus extra for dusting

70g (2½oz) vegetarian suet

seeds from 4 green cardamom
pods, crushed with a pestle
and mortar

pinch of salt

light oil (such as groundnut
or sunflower), for oiling

FOR THE FILLING

100g (3½oz) coconut sugar
or light muscovado sugar

100g (3½oz) vegan dark
chocolate chips or dark
chocolate bar chopped into
small pieces (minimum 70%
cocoa solids)

70g (2½oz) toasted flaked
almonds

2 tablespoons agave syrup
(or other syrup), plus extra
for glazing (optional)

2 tablespoons vegan cocoa
powder

1 teaspoon ground cinnamon

seeds from 2 cardamom pods,
crushed with a pestle and
mortar

The slight citrusy flavour of cardamom works particularly well with dark chocolate. It really is worth buying whole cardamom pods and crushing them with a pestle and mortar to extract the seeds from the husks, as ready-ground cardamom tends to include the husk, so the flavour is less aromatic. The crunch of the almonds is lovely, but if you're not keen or allergic, you can trade them for another nut - hazelnuts would also be great - or omit them altogether.

1 Follow the instructions for the Walnut, Date and Cinnamon Rolls opposite to make the dough.

2 To make the filling, put all the ingredients in a food processor along with 2 tablespoons of water and pulse until well combined. Alternatively, chop the chocolate quite finely and then mix everything together in a bowl.

3 Preheat the oven to 200°C (400°F), Gas Mark 6. Line a 25cm (10-inch) round springform tin with baking parchment.

4 Turn the dough out on to a floured work surface and roll out to a rectangle measuring 20 × 80cm (8 × 32 inches) and just shy of 5mm (¼ inch) thick. Sprinkle the filling evenly over the dough. Roll the dough into a log and slice into about 10 rolls, 8-10cm (3¼-4 inches) thick.

5 Lay the rolls flat in the lined tin so that the swirls are facing upwards - it's OK if they are touching. Cover with clingfilm and leave to rest at room temperature for 20 minutes. If you're making them the night before, pop them in the refrigerator at this point.

6 Brush the rolls with almond milk and bake for 20-25 minutes until risen and golden brown. If you'd like to glaze the rolls, brush them with agave syrup 5 minutes before the end of the baking. Transfer them to a wire rack to cool slightly before serving warm. These are best eaten fresh but will keep in an airtight container for up to 2 days.

BRAMLEY APPLE, APRICOT & BLUEBERRY CRUMBLE-TOP MUFFINS

Blueberry muffins are a brunch classic; these ones are unbelievably moist and keep really well. You can use shop-bought apple purée instead of making your own if you like, but it will be wetter, so use a little more flour (about 40g/1½oz or so). By reserving half the blueberries for the top, you will ensure everyone gets some and it looks lovely. You can substitute raspberries or blackberries if you prefer. For a gluten-free option, use gluten-free self-raising flour, baking powder and oats.

1 Preheat the oven to 200°C (400°F), Gas Mark 6. Line a baking tray with baking parchment or use a silicone mat.

2 Toss the prepared apples in the 75g (2¾oz) caster sugar in a bowl, then spread out on the lined tray and bake for 15-20 minutes until soft to the touch. Remove from the oven, transfer the apples to a bowl and leave to cool slightly.

3 Reduce the oven temperature to 190°C (375°F), Gas Mark 5. Line 9-10 cups of a muffin tray with muffin cases.

4 For the crumble top, measure out all the ingredients into a bowl and mix together, then pinch the mixture between your fingers until it has a crumb consistency.

5 Drain the apricots, then add to a food processor with the apples and lemon zest and pulse until you have a chunky purée. Or mash the apples with a potato masher, then finely chop the drained apricots and mix into the mashed apple with the lemon zest.

6 Cream the margarine and remaining sugar in a stand mixer fitted with the paddle attachment, or by hand with a wooden spoon in a large bowl, until pale and fluffy. Beat in the apple mixture.

7 Mix the flour and baking powder together, then fold into the muffin mixture, followed by half the blueberries.

8 Using 2 tablespoons, one to scoop and one to scrape, fill the muffin cases to about 1cm (½ inch) from the top. Scatter with the remaining blueberries (about 3 each) and the crumble top.

9 Bake the muffins for 25-30 minutes until they spring back to the touch. Leave to cool in the tray for about 5 minutes, then transfer to a wire rack to finish cooling, or serve warm. Store in an airtight container for up to 2 days.

MAKES 9-10 MUFFINS

450g (1lb) peeled and cored Bramley apples, cut into 3cm (1¼-inch) chunks

75g (2¾oz) caster sugar for baking the apples, plus 160g (5¾oz) for the muffin mixture

75g (2¾oz) dried apricots, soaked in hot water for 30 minutes

grated zest of 1 lemon

80g (3oz) vegan margarine

250g (9oz) self-raising flour

2½ teaspoons baking powder

100g (3½oz) blueberries

FOR THE CRUMBLE TOP

35g (1¼oz) self-raising flour

25g (1oz) jumbo oats

30g (1oz) demerara sugar

25g (1oz) vegan margarine, chilled

pinch of salt

BANANA, MAPLE & PECAN MUFFINS

What better use for your slightly ropey bananas than these yummy muffins – a fantastic treat for a special breakfast or afternoon snack. These can be made without refined sugar and are really low in fat compared to a lot of cakes. It is important to use ripe bananas, as under-ripe ones will be too starchy and as a consequence you'll get a much heavier, less sweet muffin. For a gluten-free option, substitute gluten-free flour and baking powder.

1   Preheat the oven to 180°C (350°F), Gas Mark 4. Line 9–10 cups of a muffin tray with muffin cases.

2   Beat the sugar, maple syrup and melted coconut oil together in a stand mixer fitted with the paddle attachment, or with a wooden spoon in a large bowl, until the sugar is beginning to dissolve (about 2–3 minutes in the mixer).

3   Add the mashed banana and beat a little more until fully incorporated.

4   Measure out the flour, baking powder, salt, cinnamon and chopped pecans into a bowl and mix to combine, then fold into the banana mixture.

5   Quickly spoon the muffin mixture into the muffin cases, filling them to about 5mm (¼ inch) from the top. Scatter with whole pecans or banana chips and a little crumbled sugar.

6   Bake the muffins for 20–25 minutes until they spring back to the touch and are making your house smell amazing! Leave to cool in the tray for about 5 minutes, then transfer to a wire rack to finish cooling, or serve warm. Store in an airtight container for up to 2 days.

MAKES 9–10 MUFFINS

160g (5¾oz) raw coconut sugar or soft light brown sugar, plus extra to crumble on top

3 tablespoons maple syrup

80g (3oz) coconut oil, melted

400g (14oz) peeled and roughly mashed ripe banana (about 4 bananas)

220g (8oz) self-raising flour

3 teaspoons baking powder

pinch of salt

1 teaspoon ground cinnamon

70g (2½oz) pecan nuts, chopped

whole pecan nuts or banana chips, to decorate

BANANA & WALNUT BREAD

SERVES 6-8

light oil (such as groundnut
or sunflower), for oiling
(optional)

2-3 tablespoons granulated
or caster sugar, for coating
the tin (optional)

160g (5¾oz) soft light brown
sugar, plus extra for the top
(optional)

80g (3oz) coconut oil, melted
(or other light oil if you prefer)

2 tablespoons maple or
agave syrup

grated zest and juice of 1 orange

350g (12oz) peeled and
roughly mashed ripe banana
(about 4 medium bananas)

180g (6¼oz) plain flour

2½ teaspoons baking powder

1 teaspoon bicarbonate of soda

70g (2½oz) walnuts, chopped,
plus extra for the top
(optional)

1 teaspoon ground cinnamon

½ teaspoon ground ginger

½ teaspoon salt

Simple enough for a child to make, banana bread is such a versatile semi-sweet cake. You can serve it warm with fruit and yogurt, cold as an afternoon snack or even warm with ice cream and chocolate sauce. The bananas really do have to be ripe, as the ripeness dictates their levels of sweetness, starch and moisture, so if they're not ripe, the cake will be much denser and less sweet. Some people like sultanas or dates in their banana bread, so feel free to add them if you wish. We like the texture of the moist bread with the odd crunchy nut and find it sweet enough as it is. Having said that, we have been known to add dark chocolate chips on occasion. For a gluten-free option, substitute gluten-free flour, baking powder and bicarbonate of soda.

1 Preheat the oven to 180°C (350°F), Gas Mark 4. Line a 1-litre (1¾-pint) loaf tin (measuring about 10 × 25cm/4 × 10 inches) with baking parchment or brush with light oil and sprinkle with the white sugar.

2 Beat the brown sugar, melted coconut oil, syrup and orange zest and juice together in a stand mixer fitted with the paddle attachment for 5 minutes or so. Alternatively, place in a large bowl and use a balloon whisk to beat vigorously.

3 Add the mashed banana and beat again for a few minutes.

4 Measure out all the dry ingredients into a bowl and stir with a balloon whisk until combined.

5 Fold the dry mixture into the banana mixture, then spoon into the prepared loaf tin. Scatter the top with a little sugar and chopped walnuts if you wish.

6 Bake for 35-40 minutes until a skewer inserted into the centre comes out clean-ish (without any uncooked mixture attached). Leave to cool in the tin for about 5 minutes, then transfer to a wire rack to finish cooling. Store in an airtight container for up to 3 days. The bread is also good toasted - best on the third day of keeping.

PAN-FRIED GIROLLES
WITH VEGAN HOLLANDAISE

Girolle mushrooms are such a fantastic colour and texture that we had to use them in our brunch menu. But you can of course use whichever seasonal mushroom you like - oyster mushrooms are also very good in this dish. We serve this on grilled sourdough (or gluten-free bread for a gluten-free option) with a little sautéed spinach on the side (see page 34).

1   To make the vegan hollandaise, blend all the ingredients together in a blender.

2   Transfer the mixture to a saucepan and warm very gently, stirring constantly - the sauce will thicken as it heats up. If it becomes too thick, thin it out with some more soya milk.

3   For the mushrooms, heat the oil in a wok or frying pan over a medium heat, add the garlic and fry for a minute, stirring. Add the mushrooms and crank the heat right up. Sauté, tossing frequently, for just a couple of minutes until they are beginning to brown and lose their bite. Season to taste with salt.

4   Place a slice of sourdough toast on each plate and drizzle with olive oil. Divide the mushrooms between the plates and top with the vegan hollandaise.

SERVES 4

3 tablespoons olive oil, plus extra for drizzling
1 garlic clove, grated
300–350g (10½–12oz) girolle mushrooms (or other wild mushrooms), washed and trimmed
slices of crusty sourdough bread, grilled on a hot griddle pan
salt

FOR THE VEGAN HOLLANDAISE
200ml (7fl oz) soya milk, plus extra for thinning if needed
200g (7oz) vegan margarine, melted
grated zest and juice of ½ orange
1 teaspoon Dijon mustard
1 teaspoon cider vinegar
½ tablespoon nutritional yeast flakes
salt and pepper

SOUTHERN SWEET POTATO & JALAPEÑO BISCUITS
WITH EARL GREY GRAVY & MAPLE—GRILLED MUSHROOMS

Biscuits and gravy is an American diner classic, but if you're not familiar with American biscuits, we're not talking about digestives and Bisto here. For the uninitiated, a biscuit in this context is very similar to a scone and is served as a sort of bread roll with savoury dishes or filled with egg or sausage rounds. Equally confusingly, Southern US gravy is more like a béchamel sauce and commonly has chunks of sausage in it. We have made a chunky Earl Grey-scented mushroom version, which includes a slug of Henderson's Relish, a spicy fruity condiment comparable in taste to Worcestershire sauce. You could use vegan Worcestershire sauce instead, if you like.

This is a filling brunch dish for which both the biscuits and gravy could be made in advance. If you're not keen on chilli heat, omit the jalapeños from the biscuits.

SOUTHERN SWEET POTATO & JALAPEÑO BISCUITS

1 Preheat the oven to 180°C (350°F), Gas Mark 4. Toss the sweet potato cubes in the oil in a bowl, spread out on a baking tray and roast for 15-20 minutes until tender. Remove from the oven and leave to cool.

2 Increase the oven temperature to 220°C (425°F), Gas Mark 7, and line a baking tray with baking parchment.

3 Sift the flour, baking powder and bicarbonate of soda together into a bowl, then add the sugar, salt, suet and margarine and mix to combine. Using your fingertips, rub the suet and margarine into the flour for about 7-8 minutes until fully incorporated.

4 Add the cooked sweet potato, jalapeño chillies and yogurt and mix together until the mixture forms a ball. Transfer the dough to a lightly floured work surface and use the palm of your hand to fold the dough on to itself a few times.

5 Pat the dough out to about 1.5cm (⅝ inch) thick. Use a floured 5cm (2-inch) round cutter to cut out your biscuits, dusting again with flour in between cuts. Place the biscuits on the lined baking tray, making sure the biscuits are touching each other slightly, as this will help them rise together uniformly. Knead the scraps of leftover dough again and cut to size until you have 8 biscuits.

>>

SERVES 8

SOUTHERN SWEET POTATO AND JALAPEÑO BISCUITS
100g (3½oz) sweet potatoes, peeled and diced into 2.5cm (1-inch) cubes

2 tablespoons sunflower oil, or enough to coat the sweet potatoes

280g (10oz) plain flour, plus extra for dusting

4 teaspoons baking powder

¼ teaspoon bicarbonate of soda

½ tablespoon sugar

½ teaspoon salt

40g (1½oz) vegetarian suet

40g (1½oz) vegan margarine, plus extra, melted, for glazing

50g (1¾oz) jalapeño chillies, diced

200ml (7fl oz) soya yogurt

EARL GREY GRAVY
75g (2¾oz) vegan margarine

2 shallots, finely diced

5 garlic cloves, crushed or finely grated

300g (10½oz) chestnut mushrooms, chopped

2½ tablespoons plain flour

½ teaspoon Arbol chilli flakes (optional; if you don't have these, use other chilli flakes or paprika)

6 Brush the tops of the biscuits with melted margarine to glaze and bake for 15-18 minutes until they have risen and are golden in colour. Remove from the oven, transfer to a wire rack and leave to cool for 10-15 minutes before serving.

EARL GREY GRAVY

1 Melt and heat up the margarine in a medium-sized saucepan, add the shallots and garlic and gently sauté for a few minutes, stirring frequently, until they have lost their bite. Then add the mushrooms and cook over a medium-high heat, stirring, until browned.

2 Add the flour and mix through, then stir in all the remaining ingredients. Cook, stirring constantly, until the taste of the flour is cooked out and the gravy has thickened. Add any juices left over from cooking the mushrooms (*see* below) for extra flavour.

MAPLE-GRILLED MUSHROOMS

1 Preheat the oven to 180°C (350°F), Gas Mark 4.

2 Mix the maple syrup, olive oil, tamari or soy sauce, garlic, thyme and mustard powder together in a large bowl, add the mushrooms and toss to coat. Cover with clingfilm and leave to marinate at room temperature for 30 minutes (transfer to the refrigerator if leaving for longer).

3 Heat a griddle pan until it is evenly medium hot, add the mushrooms, in batches, and cook for 3 minutes on each side, transferring each batch to a baking tray in the oven while you finish cooking the others. Cook in the oven for about 5-10 minutes until softened.

TO SERVE

1 Cut each biscuit in half and serve with a maple-grilled mushroom, along with some sautéed spinach (*see* page 34) or kale, topped with a large serving spoonful of gravy.

250ml (9fl oz) freshly brewed
  Earl Grey tea
350ml (18fl oz) oat milk
  (or other good-quality
  plant-based milk)
50ml (2fl oz) oat cream (or
  other plant-based cream)
5 tablespoons bourbon
  (optional)
2 tablespoons Henderson's
  Relish
salt and pepper

MAPLE-GRILLED
  MUSHROOMS
50ml (2fl oz) maple syrup
50ml (2fl oz) olive oil
50ml (2fl oz) tamari (gluten-
  free) or soy sauce
2 garlic cloves, crushed or
  finely grated
1 tablespoon chopped thyme
1½ teaspoons mustard powder
8 portobello mushrooms,
  washed or brushed and
  trimmed

SMOKY BAKED BEANS ON GRILLED SOURDOUGH

SERVES 4-6

250g (9oz) dried cannellini
  beans
splash of sunflower oil
1 white onion, finely diced
2 celery sticks, finely diced
1 tablespoon chopped thyme
2 bay leaves
2 × 400g (14oz) cans chopped
  tomatoes
800ml (28fl oz) water
100ml (3½fl oz) maple syrup
1 vegetable stock cube,
  crumbled
½ teaspoon liquid smoke
¼ teaspoon ground black
  pepper
salt

TO SERVE
slices of crusty sourdough
  bread, grilled on a hot
  griddle pan
olive oil

Posh baked beans (*see photograph overleaf*) are a real crowd-pleaser because they are both filling and delicious, and basically, who doesn't love beans on toast? We have amazing wood-burning ovens in our Kings Cross and Camden branches that we use to make these baked beans. To replicate that strong smoky flavour at home, we suggest using liquid smoke, which is simply water that has been filtered through wood charcoal. Try the Living Nutritionals brand (not the kind with additives), which is available from some supermarkets and online. Alternatively, cook the beans in a heavy casserole over a low-burning barbecue for a similar effect.

We like to use cannellini beans, or pinto, but you could use the traditional haricot bean if you prefer. Serve on gluten-free bread for a gluten-free option.

1   Soak the dried beans preferably overnight in plenty of cold water. Otherwise, soak them in boiling water for at least a few hours. Drain and rinse the beans, then cook in a large saucepan of lightly salted boiling water until they are fully cooked - this can take up to an hour.

2   While the beans are cooking, prepare the vegetables. Heat the oil in a frying pan, add the onion and sweat over a gentle heat for 7-8 minutes until they become translucent. Add the celery and herbs and cook for a further few minutes to give the onion some colour.

3   Blend 1 can of chopped tomatoes in a blender until puréed. Add to the frying pan with the other can of tomatoes and all the remaining ingredients and ½ teaspoon salt, bring to a simmer and cook for 10-12 minutes. Remove from the heat and set aside.

4   Preheat the oven to 190°C (375°F), Gas Mark 5.

5   Once the beans are cooked, drain and add them to the sauce, then transfer to an ovenproof dish and bake, uncovered, for 45 minutes-1 hour, stirring them occasionally, until the sauce has reduced and thickened up slightly.

6   Serve with grilled crusty sourdough, drizzled with olive oil.

THE FULL VEGAN

The ultimate hangover cure, second only to a good Bloody Mary, has to be a slap-up big breakfast. For our Full Vegan plate (*see* photograph on previous page), we serve these slow-cooked vine tomatoes, grilled portobello mushrooms and sautéed spinach with Scrambled Tofu (*see* opposite), our house Smoky Baked Beans (*see* page 31) and our vegan sausages (*see* page 81), all with a wedge of sourdough toast.

SLOW-COOKED TOMATOES

1   Preheat the oven to 140°C (275°F), Gas Mark 1. Line a baking tray with baking parchment.
2   Place the vine tomatoes on the lined baking tray and cut into stems of 3 or 4. Drizzle with a little olive oil and scatter with the oregano leaves and salt.
3   Bake for 45 minutes–1 hour until deep in colour but not collapsing.

SAUTÉED SPINACH

1   Heat the oil in a wok over a medium heat, add the garlic and stir-fry for a minute.
2   Add the spinach and toss over a medium-high heat for 1-2 minutes until it collapses, then season to taste with sea salt.

GRILLED PORTOBELLO MUSHROOMS

1   Toss the mushrooms in olive oil to coat in a bowl, then season to taste with salt and pepper.
2   Heat a griddle pan over a medium-high heat until hot, or use the frying pan you used for frying the sausages (*see* below), and sear for 3 minutes on each side until fully cooked. Remove from the pan and keep warm in the oven until ready to serve.

TO SERVE

1   Following the instructions on page 81, fry the sausages and then transfer to the oven to finish cooking while you cook the mushrooms (*see* above). Meanwhile, heat up the scrambled tofu (*see* instructions opposite) and baked beans (either in the oven with the sausages or in a small saucepan on the hob), then serve with the sautéed spinach, mushrooms, tomatoes, sausages and toasted sourdough.

SERVES AS MANY AS YOU WANT

SLOW-COOKED TOMATOES
cherry tomatoes on the vine, 3 or 4 per person
olive oil
2–3 sprigs of oregano, leaves picked
sea salt flakes

SAUTÉED SPINACH
splash of olive oil
½ small garlic clove per person, crushed
1 handful of large leaf spinach per person, washed
sea salt flakes

GRILLED PORTOBELLO MUSHROOMS
2 small or baby portobello mushrooms per person, washed or brushed and trimmed
olive oil
salt and pepper

TO SERVE
Smoked Tofu and White Bean Sausages (*see* page 81)
Scrambled Tofu (*see* opposite)
Smoky Baked Beans (*see* page 31)
slices of sourdough bread, toasted

SERVES 4

325g (11½oz) pack firm tofu

¼ teaspoon turmeric

⅛ teaspoon ground black salt

⅛ teaspoon garlic powder
   (optional)

pinch of ground white pepper

about 50ml (2fl oz) vegan
   single cream, if reheating

salt

SCRAMBLED TOFU

Scrambled tofu is the vegan answer to scrambled eggs. It's been around for ages and was all over menus at hippy places in the USA twenty years ago, but it now seems to be popping up everywhere as a vegan brunch option. Our recipe calls for black salt, which confusingly isn't black in colour but has a high sulphur content and therefore lends the dish a suitably eggy flavour. We serve this as part of our Full Vegan (*see* opposite), but you can also serve it with our Southern Sweet Potato and Jalapeño Biscuits (*see* page 28) or gluten-free bread for a gluten-free option.

1   Preheat the oven to 180°C (350°F), Gas Mark 4. Line a baking tray with baking parchment (or use a nonstick baking tray).

2   Put all the ingredients in a bowl and crush together with your hands until the seasoning is evenly distributed and the tofu is in small chunks.

3   Spread the mixture out on the lined baking tray and bake for 10-15 minutes. Serve immediately from the oven, but if needing to reheat, put the scrambled tofu in a small saucepan or frying pan and add enough vegan single cream to make it moist, then warm through gently, stirring.

STARTERS & SOUPS

CASHEW & SMOKED TOFU POTSTICKER GYOZA

Consistently one of our most popular starters, dumplings fly out of the doors at Mildreds (see photographs overleaf). They aren't complicated to assemble; even the wrappers aren't too tricky to make – or you can buy them pre-made at Asian grocery stores. Unlike wonton wrappers, which usually contain egg, gyoza wrappers are vegan, simply consisting of plain flour and warm water. The filling must be relatively dry but otherwise it's open to various options, so you can swap the smoked tofu for regular firm tofu, add more spice or change the cashews for peanuts.

Once assembled and before cooking, the dumplings can be frozen, by first open freezing on a tray to prevent them from sticking together and then packing into bags to store. Defrost before cooking or cook from frozen and cook for 2–3 minutes longer.

1   First make the filling. Pulse the cashews in a food processor to a crunchy crumb consistency. Remove to a bowl. Without washing the food processor bowl, add the tofu and pulse to a mince-like texture, then add to the bowl. Alternatively, chop the cashews by hand to a crunchy crumb consistency, and crush the tofu with your hands until roughly crumbled.

2   Pulse all the other filling ingredients in the food processor to very small chunks. Alternatively, chop by hand very finely to a chunky mash. Add to the cashews and tofu and stir to combine.

3   Transfer the filling mixture to a sieve set over a bowl. Cover and then leave to drain in the refrigerator for between 5–12 hours.

4   To assemble the gyoza, wet the edges of a wrapper with a pastry brush dipped in water, place a teaspoon of filling in the centre of the wrapper and then pinch the edges of the wrapper together to enclose the filling. Sit the dumpling on its base and plump down to flatten the bottom. Place on a tray lined with baking parchment. Continue until all the filling is used. Cover and keep in the refrigerator until you are ready to cook them.

>>

MAKES 16–20 GYOZA; SERVES 4

15–20 gyoza wrappers
sesame oil and vegetable oil, for frying
75–100ml (2⅓–3½fl oz) warm or boiling water

FOR THE FILLING
75g (2¾oz) roasted, salted cashew nuts
150g (5½oz) smoked tofu
50g (1¾oz) Chinese cabbage or pak choi, roughly chopped
2 spring onions, chopped
½ small carrot, peeled and grated
20g (¾oz) bean sprouts
6 sprigs of coriander, leaves picked
½ small red chilli
1–2 garlic cloves, grated
1 teaspoon peeled and grated fresh root ginger
1 tablespoon tamari (gluten-free) or dark soy sauce
1 tablespoon sweet chilli sauce
1 tablespoon sesame oil

FOR THE DIP

4 tablespoons sweet
  chilli sauce

3 tablespoons tamari (gluten-
  free) or dark soy sauce

2 tablespoons rice vinegar
  or sushi seasoning

TO GARNISH

finely sliced spring onions

coriander leaves

toasted black and white
  sesame seeds (optional)

5 To cook the gyoza, you can either steam or fry them, but we use a potsticker method that is a mixture of the two. For this you will need a large (28cm/11-inch) nonstick frying pan and a lid big enough to cover it. Heat the pan with a slug each of sesame oil and vegetable oil. Add the dumplings to the pan, however many will fit in a single layer, bottoms down and close together but not touching. Cook over a medium heat until the bases are an even golden colour. Add the measured warm or boiling water and bring up to a simmer before covering the pan with the lid. Steam for about 2–3 minutes until the dumpling wrappers are becoming fairly translucent. Uncover and continuing cooking for a further 2–3 minutes until the water has evaporated and the bases are crunchy. Remove and keep warm in the oven while you repeat with the remaining gyoza.

6 Meanwhile, to make the dip, combine all the ingredients thoroughly in a serving bowl.

7 Serve the gyoza with the dip, scattered with finely sliced spring onions, coriander leaves and toasted sesame seeds, if liked.

PISTACHIO & ALMOND FETA KIBBEH

According to a great Syrian cookbook we have, you can tell the skill of a cook by how thin and delicate their kibbeh shells are. A Middle Eastern dish made using bulgur (cracked) wheat with a fragrantly spiced filling, they are so popular in their native region that Kenwood actually sell a special attachment for making kibbeh shells. We keep it "old school" and make them by hand.

Our filling is minced seitan with the addition of pistachios and vegan feta to give this dish a great flavour. Seitan is pure wheat gluten, extracted from wheat flour by washing it until all the starch has been removed, then seasoned and cooked before use.

Paired with Tahini Sauce (see page 144) and Ezme Salad (see page 162), these make a great starter (see photograph overleaf). Alternatively, you can serve them simply with a side of minted yogurt.

1   Put the bulgur wheat in a bowl, add the measured hot water, cover with clingfilm and leave to stand for at least 40 minutes until the water has been absorbed.

2   Meanwhile, make the filling. Put the seitan in a food processor and pulse until it resembles fine mince, or chop it finely by hand.

3   Heat the oil in a frying pan and sauté the onion over a medium heat, stirring frequently, until translucent. Add the garlic and chilli and cook, stirring, for a couple of minutes. Add all the spices and mint and cook for a further few minutes, stirring, until the spices release their aroma. Add the minced seitan and mix together well, then season to taste with salt and pepper.

4   Remove from the heat and leave to cool slightly, then stir in the almond feta, pistachios and parsley until well combined. Set aside.

5   Once the bulgur has absorbed the water, add the flour, sumac, salt and cumin. Using your hands, work the bulgur into a pliable mixture that holds together, adding a couple of tablespoons of water to help bind it.

>>

MAKES 8–10 KIBBEH; SERVES 4–6

150ml (5fl oz) vegetable oil, for frying the kibbeh

FOR THE SHELLS
200g (7oz) bulgur wheat
250ml (9fl oz) hot water
3 tablespoons self-raising flour
1 tablespoon sumac
½ teaspoon salt
¼ teaspoon ground cumin

FOR THE FILLING
120g (4¼oz) seitan
splash of vegetable oil
½ onion, finely diced
2 garlic cloves, crushed
1 small green chilli, finely diced
1 teaspoon ground allspice
1 teaspoon ground coriander
¼ teaspoon ground cinnamon
1 teaspoon dried mint
100g (3½oz) Almond Feta (see page 242)
30g (1oz) raw shelled pistachio nuts
30g (1oz) flat leaf parsley, chopped
salt and pepper

TO SERVE
Tahini Sauce (*see* page 144)
Ezme Salad (*see* page 162)

6 To shape the kibbeh, scoop a heaped tablespoon of the bulgur mixture on to the palm of your hand and firmly pat out to form a thin layer big enough to cover most of your palm. With your free hand, take about a large teaspoon of the seitan mixture and compress it in the palm of your hand until well compacted, then place in the centre of the bulgur. Close your hand to make a fist so that the bulgur wraps itself around the seitan mixture and squeeze down to compress it into an oval or round ball. If you can still see some exposed seitan mixture, patch up the shell with a little more bulgur wheat. The layer of bulgur wheat must be as thin as possible to enable a quick cooking time and achieve a light kibbeh. Repeat this process so that you end up with 8-10 small egg-sized kibbeh.

7 Heat the oil for frying the kibbeh in a large (28cm/11-inch) frying pan over a medium heat until it reaches about 180°C (350°F) or until a cube of bread browns in 30 seconds. Add the kibbeh, in small batches, and fry for about 4-5 minutes, turning them so that all sides become golden. Drain the kibbeh from the pan on to kitchen paper to absorb the excess oil.

8 Serve hot, drizzled with tahini sauce, along with ezme salad.

BUFFALO–MARINATED TOFU
WITH CRUNCHY CRUMB COATING

Based on the American bar classic buffalo wings, this crunchy spicy tofu is the perfect companion to cold beer. You can dial down the heat level by reducing the amount of chilli sauce, though the heat is authentic, and that way you have to drink more beer to cool off. We serve this with cold celery and carrot crudités along with our vegan Ranch Dip (*see* page 174).

1   Cut the tofu into 10-12 cubes or 6-7 slabs - the shape and size is up to you. Place in a bowl.

2   Combine the remaining ingredients, except the oil for frying, in a small saucepan and heat over a medium heat, stirring, until the mixture begins to simmer. Pour the hot marinade over the tofu pieces and leave to cool, then cover with clingfilm and leave to marinate in the refrigerator for at least 12 and up to 24 hours.

3   Preheat the oven to 190°C (375°F), Gas Mark 5.

4   Remove the tofu from the marinade, then strain and reserve the marinade liquid to use for crumbing the tofu.

5   Place the tofu pieces on a baking tray, spacing them out well to allow them to cook properly, and bake for 15-20 minutes until they have firmed up slightly and have turned golden brown. Remove from the oven and leave to cool.

6   For the crumb coating, mix the soya cream into the leftover marinade. Put the lightly seasoned flour in a separate bowl and the breadcrumbs in another. Begin to crumb the tofu pieces by first dipping them into the flour, then the marinade sauce and finally the breadcrumbs.

7   Heat the oil for frying the tofu in a large (28cm/11-inch) frying pan over a medium heat until it reaches about 180°C (350°F) or until a cube of bread browns in 30 seconds. Add the tofu pieces, in batches, and fry for about 2 minutes on each side until they are golden. Drain the tofu from the pan on to kitchen paper to absorb the excess oil.

8   Serve hot with the ranch dip and the celery and carrot batons.

SERVES 4

325g (11½oz) pack firm tofu

40g (1½oz) soya margarine

100g (3½oz) Lingham's Extra Hot Chilli Sauce or Frank's RedHot Original Cayenne Pepper Sauce, or your favourite hot sauce

30g (1oz) sriracha chilli sauce

2 tablespoons Henderson's Relish (*see* page 28)

1 tablespoon cider vinegar

1½ teaspoons garlic powder

200ml (7fl oz) vegetable oil, for frying

FOR THE CRUMB COATING

50ml (2fl oz) soya cream

60g (2¼oz) plain flour, lightly seasoned with salt and pepper

120g (4¼oz) panko breadcrumbs

TO SERVE

Ranch Dip (*see* page 174)

2 celery sticks, peeled and sliced into thin batons

2 carrots, peeled and sliced into thin batons

SEITAN LAHMAJUNS
WITH CUCUMBER SALAD

MAKES 6 LAHMAJUNS

½ × 7g (⅓oz) sachet
  fast-action dried yeast

75ml (2½fl oz) warm water

2 tablespoons olive oil,
  plus extra for oiling

1 teaspoon caster sugar

175g (6oz) strong white flour,
  plus extra for dusting

Tahini Sauce (*see* page 144)
  or Hummus (*see* page 175),
  to serve

FOR THE TOPPING

150g (5½oz) seitan

1 tablespoon vegetable oil

1 small onion, diced

½ red chilli, diced

1 large garlic clove, crushed

2 teaspoons Baharat Spice Mix
  (*see* page 194)

½ tablespoon Middle Eastern
  black tamarind concentrate

½ tablespoon tomato purée

1 tomato, deseeded and diced

½ teaspoon soft dark brown
  sugar

15g (½oz) flat leaf parsley,
  chopped

15g (½oz) coriander, chopped

20g (¾oz) roasted pine nuts

salt

Most British people are used to seeing the large Turkish lahmajuns in Meze Mangal restaurants. Sometimes called Turkish pizza, the name comes from the Arabic *lahm bi ajeen*, or 'bread with meat'. The traditional mince is replaced here with minced seitan, which provides a very similar texture and flavour. These are closer in texture and taste to the smaller, softer Syrian and Egyptian type of lahmajun that is flavoured with strong black Arabic tamarind concentrate. Lahmajuns are almost like an edible plate on to which salad, hummus, pickles and tahini sauce can be piled.

1   Mix the yeast with the measured warm water, olive oil and sugar in a large bowl. Cover with clingfilm and leave somewhere fairly warm to activate for about 15 minutes until beginning to froth.

2   Add half the flour to the yeast mixture and whisk together with a fork, then mix in the rest of the flour.

3   Oil a work surface with olive oil, then turn the dough out and knead for 8-10 minutes until smooth. Return to the bowl, cover with clingfilm and leave to rise in a warm place for 30 minutes. Turn the dough back out and knead for 2 minutes, then return to the bowl again, cover and leave to rise for 30 minutes.

4   In between kneads, make the topping. Dice the seitan into small cubes, place in a food processor and pulse until it resembles large grains of rice, then set aside.

5   Heat the vegetable oil in a small saucepan, add the onion and fry over a medium heat, stirring frequently, for 5 minutes until beginning to colour. Add the chilli and garlic and cook for a further few minutes until the onion is soft and translucent. Add the spice mix and seitan and cook for a minute, stirring, until the spices release their aroma.

6   Add the tamarind, tomato purée, tomato and sugar and cook over a low heat for 8-10 minutes. Remove from hob and leave to cool, then add the chopped herbs and pine nuts, and season to taste with salt if needed (seitan can be quite salty).

>>

FOR THE CUCUMBER
SALAD

½ cucumber, peeled
  and deseeded

½ small red onion

¼ iceberg lettuce

30g (1oz) flat leaf parsley,
  chopped

2 tablespoons lemon juice

2 tablespoons olive oil

salt (if needed)

7   Divide the dough into 6 small balls and roll out into discs about 5mm (¼ inch) thick. Transfer to 2 large, floured baking trays. Top each dough disc with a very thin layer of the seitan mixture and leave to rest while you preheat the oven to 220°C (425°F), Gas Mark 7.

8   Bake the lahmajuns for 10-15 minutes until golden on the edges and the base is crisp.

9   Meanwhile, make the salad. Slice or dice the cucumber and finely dice the red onion. Dice or finely shred the lettuce. Combine all the ingredients in a bowl and dress with the lemon juice and olive oil just before serving.

10   Serve the lahmajuns hot with the cucumber salad and tahini sauce or hummus.

BUTTERNUT SQUASH & PISTACHIO BOREK

Boreks are Middle Eastern or Turkish pies made with filo pastry and, as most shop-bought filo pastry is vegan, this is a simple starter to make. The sweetness of the roast squash and caramelized onion pairs well with the salty crunchy nuts. We make the filling quite thin so that the moisture in the squash doesn't turn the pastry soft. You can use pumpkin instead, though I would stick to a starchier variety, not the wet Halloween-style pumpkin. We serve this with Sautéed Spinach with Golden Sultanas and Salted Pistachios (*see* page 160).

1   Preheat the oven to 200°C (400°F), Gas Mark 6.
2   Mix the squash with the garlic, thyme, spice mix and olive oil in a large bowl, making sure it is well coated. Spread out on a baking tray and roast for 20-25 minutes until fully cooked.
3   While the squash is cooking, caramelize the onions. Heat the blended oil in a frying pan, add the onions and cook over a medium heat, stirring occasionally, for 10-15 minutes until golden brown. Add the sugar and cook for a further 5-8 minutes or until the onions are dark golden.
4   Put the nuts in a bowl or on to a clean tea towel and use a rolling pin or similar blunt instrument to crush them slightly, then set aside.
5   Remove the roasted squash from the oven once it is done, and reduce the oven temperature slightly to 190°C (375°F), Gas Mark 5. Line a baking tray with parchment paper.
6   Cut the sheets of pastry in half across to make 2 rectangles from each sheet. Keep the rectangles covered in clingfilm or baking parchment with a damp clean tea towel over the top. Brush one rectangle with a little melted margarine, then brush another and lay it on top to double the thickness. Place a small amount of the roasted squash, caramelized onion and crushed nuts in the centre of the pastry. Fold in the sides over the filling. Then fold the bottom up over the filling and continue folding the pastry over on to itself to form a closed parcel. You should get around 6 parcels, depending on the size of the pastry sheets.
7   Place the parcels on the baking tray, brush the tops with the rest of the melted margarine and sprinkle with any remaining nuts.
8   Bake for 25-30 minutes until golden brown. Serve hot with the spinach, if liked.

MAKES ABOUT 6 BOREKS

700g (1lb 9oz) butternut squash, peeled, deseeded and cut into thin slices or small cubes

2 garlic cloves, finely chopped or grated

6 sprigs of thyme, leaves picked and chopped (1 tablespoon)

2 teaspoons Baharat Spice Mix (*see* page 194) or shop-bought Lebanese seven spice mix

2 tablespoons olive oil

1 tablespoon blended oil (olive and sunflower or light olive oil)

500g (1lb 2oz) onions, sliced

1 tablespoon soft dark brown sugar

60g (2¼oz) salted shelled pistachio nuts (*see* page 57 for homemade)

40g (1½oz) salted blanched almonds

225g (8oz) filo pastry, defrosted if frozen

100g (3½oz) vegan margarine, melted

Sautéed Spinach with Golden Sultanas and Salted Pistachios (*see* page 160), to serve (optional)

BLACK RICE, PETIT POIS & EDAMAME ROLLS
WITH WASABI AVOCADO CREAM

The black rice in these nori rolls, which is in fact a very deep purple colour, looks amazing with the bright green edamame and petit pois, and the pale green avocado cream.

You can prepare the filling and rice in advance, but not too far ahead as the rice will harden, so cook and use the same day. Roll the nori just before serving to avoid it becoming soft and chewy.

1   Cook the rice according to the packet instructions until tender. Drain and leave to cool completely. Add a small splash of sesame oil and tamari or dark soy sauce to the rice and toss to coat.

2   Heat the 2 tablespoons sesame oil in a frying pan, add the chilli and ginger and fry over a medium-high heat for 3 minutes, stirring, until fragrant. Add the spring onions and fry, stirring frequently, for 2–3 minutes until softened. Add the petit pois and edamame and heat through for a minute, stirring. Add the coriander, tamari or dark soy sauce, sweet chilli sauce and sesame seeds and cook for another minute or so.

3   Remove from the heat and drain in a fine sieve. Turn out on to a chopping board and chop a little with a large knife, just enough to break up the edamame and petit pois slightly.

4   To make the wasabi avocado cream, halve the avocado and remove the stone and skin. Add the flesh to a blender with the other ingredients, or use a stick blender, and process until smooth (if the mixture is too thick, add a little water or coconut water).

5   To assemble the rolls, place the nori on a bamboo rolling mat if you have one. If not, just use a clean, dry work surface. Divide the rice and the filling into the desired number of rolls – between 6–8 depending on the size of the nori sheets. Cover the bottom half of a nori sheet with a thin layer of rice and then add a small teaspoon of wasabi cream along the width of the rice. Next, place a ½ teaspoon-thick layer of the edamame mixture down the centre of the rice. Slightly wet the top edge of the nori sheet and then roll very tightly. When you have made all the rolls, use a sharp serrated knife to cut each roll into 5–6 pieces.

6   Serve with the wasabi avocado cream and pickled ginger, garnished with finely sliced spring onions.

MAKES 30–48 PIECES

125g (4½oz) black rice, washed

2 tablespoons sesame oil, plus extra for adding to the rice

2 tablespoons tamari (gluten-free) or dark soy sauce, plus extra for adding to the rice

1 red chilli, very finely chopped

10g (¼oz) fresh root ginger, peeled and very finely chopped

6 spring onions, very finely chopped

100g (3½oz) petit pois

100g (3½oz) shelled edamame beans

20g (¾oz) coriander leaves, chopped

2 tablespoons sweet chilli sauce

2 tablespoons toasted black sesame seeds

6–8 sheets of nori seaweed

FOR THE WASABI AVOCADO CREAM

1 large ripe Hass avocado

juice of 1 lime

1–2 tablespoons wasabi paste

220ml (8fl oz) light coconut milk

salt

TO SERVE

finely sliced spring onions

pickled ginger

CHARRED LEEKS & PEPPERS
WITH CRISPY POLENTA & SMOKED CHILLI JAM

SERVES 4

The leeks and peppers in this recipe are best cooked over a charcoal barbecue, but a hot gas barbecue or even a griddle pan on the hob indoors can be used.

1   Once the flames of your charcoal barbecue have died down and the coals are glowing, add the leeks and peppers directly to the hot coals. Cook the leeks for 5–6 minutes on each side until they have blackened and begun to caramelize. Cook the peppers for 2–3 minutes on each side until the skins are blistered and blackened, then move them to a cooler part of the barbecue to cook until the flesh softens. Remove the peppers to a bowl and cover with clingfilm. Set the leeks aside. Leave to cool.

2   Alternatively, if you are cooking indoors, preheat the oven to 200°C (400°F), Gas Mark 6. Heat a griddle pan on the hob over a medium-high heat. Brush the vegetables with a little sunflower oil. Add the leeks to the pan and cook until they have blackened, turning every 4–5 minutes. Remove from the pan to a baking tray. Repeat this process with the peppers and add to the tray with the leeks. Roast for 15–20 minutes until the leeks are soft and fully cooked and the flesh of the peppers has softened up slightly. Remove from the oven and leave the vegetables to cool.

3   Once cool, cut the peppers in half and remove and discard the seeds and charred skin. Slice the leeks lengthways and peel off the charred outer skin. Cut the vegetables into large chunks.

4   For the polenta, line a small baking tray with greaseproof paper. Add the sweetcorn kernels to a blender and blitz to a paste.

5   Transfer the sweetcorn paste to a small saucepan with the measured water, crumbled stock cube, yeast flakes and salt and bring to the boil, stirring. Using a balloon whisk, whisk in the polenta and continue to whisk constantly for 2–3 minutes until the polenta is fully cooked. Spread the polenta on to the lined baking tray to a thickness of about 1.5cm (⁵⁄₈ inch). Leave to cool.

6   Once the polenta has cooled, use a 6cm (2½-inch) cookie cutter or rim of a glass to cut it into discs, or cut into triangles with a knife. Heat the vegetable oil in a large frying pan, add the polenta shapes and fry over a medium heat for 3–4 minutes on each side until they turn crispy and brown. Serve along with the charred vegetables, either at room temperature or heated up in a pan, along with some rocket and a good dollop of the chilli jam.

3 leeks, trimmed and washed
4 red peppers
sunflower oil, for brushing
   (if cooking indoors)

FOR THE POLENTA
100g (3½oz) sweetcorn kernels
700ml (1¼ pints) water
1 vegetable stock cube
2½ tablespoons yeast flakes
¼ teaspoon salt
150g (5½oz) quick-cook
   polenta
splash of vegetable oil

TO SERVE
rocket
Smoked Chilli Jam (*see*
   page 180)

TAMARIND-GLAZED BEETROOT

WITH BABY SPINACH, SALTED PISTACHIOS & SOYA LABNEH

SERVES 6

FOR THE BAKED BEETROOT

6 medium beetroot, trimmed

1 orange, quartered

4 sprigs of rosemary

3 garlic cloves

drizzle of olive oil

FOR THE SALTED PISTACHIOS

50g (1¾oz) salt

100ml (3½fl oz) warm water

200g (7oz) raw shelled pistachio nuts

FOR THE TAMARIND GLAZE

4 tablespoons agave syrup

3 tablespoons Middle Eastern black tamarind concentrate

½ tablespoon toasted and coarsely crushed cumin seeds

½ teaspoon sumac

TO FINISH

splash of olive oil

2 garlic cloves, thinly sliced

¼ red chilli, thinly sliced

200g (7oz) baby spinach, washed

about 200g (7oz) Soya Labneh, about 1 tablespoon per person (*see* page 246)

We strongly recommend that you bake the beetroot for this recipe according to the instructions below - baked beetroot have a stronger flavour, deeper colour and a denser, crunchier texture. Having said that, you could use boiled and it will still taste really nice. We use regular purple beetroot, but do try multicoloured ones if you wish. And if you don't have time to make the labneh, you could use a smear of oat crème fraîche. See the photographs on the following pages for inspiration!

1   Preheat the oven to 180°C (350°F), Gas Mark 4.

2   Cut a piece of foil large enough to wrap the beetroot and an equally large piece of baking parchment. Place the foil on a baking tray and top with the baking parchment. Put the beetroot and the other ingredients for the baked beetroot on top and then wrap the parchment and foil around to seal tightly. Bake for 1½ hours.

3   Remove from the oven and set aside to cool, leaving the oven on. Peel and cut the beetroot in half and then into wedges, yielding about 6 wedges per beetroot (discard the orange and aromatics).

4   While the beetroot are cooling, make the salted pistachios. Add the salt to the measured warm water in a bowl and stir until dissolved. Add the nuts and leave to soak for a few minutes. Line a baking sheet with baking parchment.

5   Using a slotted spoon, scoop the nuts on to the lined baking sheet and spread out, then bake for 15-20 minutes at the same oven temperature as for the beetroot. Remove, leave to cool and then crush slightly. (Store what you don't use, or if making in advance, in an airtight container.)

6   To make the glaze, combine all the ingredients in a small bowl.

7   To finish, heat the olive oil in a wok, add the garlic and chilli and fry over a medium-high heat for 1 minute, stirring. Add the baked beetroot and about 1 tablespoon of the glaze and toss over a high heat for about 1 minute until coated.

8   Transfer the beetroot to a large bowl, add the baby spinach and toss together. Drizzle tamarind glaze on each plate and then add a smear of the soya labneh. Add a pile of the beetroot and spinach mixture, topping off with the salted pistachios.

BABY KALE SALAD
WITH SMOKED ALMONDS, TOASTED CRUMBS & VEGAN CAESAR DRESSING

We recently came across salad crumbs on a development trip to California. They are delicious ground croutons, which means you get loads of crunch all the way through your salad, not just in chunks. Baby kale is really lovely if you can find it, but if you can't you can substitute other baby greens or salad leaves. Alternatively, use regular kale stripped of its tough stems and torn into small pieces. Squeeze over a little lemon juice and sprinkle lightly with salt, then work through the kale with your hands and leave to sit for an hour and it will become very tender.

1   If you can't find smoked almonds, first prepare your almonds. Preheat the oven to 180°C (350°F), Gas Mark 4. Line a baking sheet with baking parchment. Mix together the unblanched almonds, syrup, liquid smoke and salt to taste in a bowl, then spread out on the lined baking sheet. Bake for 10-15 minutes until dry, stirring occasionally. Remove from the oven and leave to cool.

2   For the crumbs, preheat the oven to 190°C (375°F), Gas Mark 5.

3   Toss the bread cubes with the herb oil and salt in a bowl. Spread out on a baking tray and bake for 10-15 minutes, stirring occasionally, until you have very crunchy croutons.

4   Remove from the oven and leave to cool, then pulse in the food processor a few times to break up into large crumbs.

5   Transfer the almonds to a chopping board and use a chopping knife to cut up into rough slivers.

6   To assemble, toss the kale with the dressing and the almonds in a bowl. Just before serving, sprinkle the crumbs over the top (don't do this in advance, as they will go soggy).

SERVES 4 AS A STARTER OR 6 AS A SIDE

30g (1oz) smoked almonds – if you can't find smoked almonds, use the following (*see* first step of method): 30g (1oz) whole unblanched almonds, 2 tablespoons maple syrup (or other syrup), ½ teaspoon liquid smoke (*see* page 31), salt

150g (5½oz) baby kale

150-175ml (5-6fl oz) Vegan Caesar Dressing (*see* page 184)

salt

FOR THE CRUMBS

125g (4½oz) sourdough or similar bread, cut into 2.5cm (1-inch) cubes

50ml (2fl oz) Herb Oil (*see* page 186)

large pinch of sea salt flakes

WARM RED CHICORY, RADISH & BRUSSELS SPROUT SALAD
WITH ROAST GARLIC AIOLI

SERVES 4–6

400g (14oz) Brussels sprouts

500g (1lb 2oz) red chicory
(about 3 large)

juice of 1 orange

large pinch of sea salt flakes

50ml (2fl oz) Herb Oil (*see*
page 186), or 50ml (2fl oz)
light olive oil and ½ teaspoon
chopped thyme leaves and
1 garlic clove, sliced, shaken
together in a screw-top jar

6 spring onions, thinly sliced

4 radishes, thinly sliced

½ bunch of chives, cut into 2cm
(¾-inch) batons

100ml (3½fl oz) Roast Garlic
Aioli (*see* page 181) – if it's
quite thick, loosen with a little
orange juice or soya milk

Roasting chicory (also known as endive) and Brussels sprouts draws out the natural sweetness in these vegetables. Having seen a renaissance in the last few years, the humble Brussels sprout is now all over the menus of chic restaurants in the USA. If you can't get red chicory, then you can use the regular variety or even spring greens, cavolo nero (black kale) or kale instead.

1   Preheat the oven to 190°C (375°F), Gas Mark 5.

2   Trim the bases of the sprouts and remove and discard all the tough outer leaves, then cut in half. Wash and drain.

3   Peel away and discard the thicker outer leaves of the chicory, as these can be quite bitter. Cut in half lengthways and then slice each half into 5, cutting out from the core so that the core holds the slices together.

4   Toss the chicory and sprouts with the orange juice, salt and oil in a large bowl. Turn out into a baking tray and spread out, then roast for 15–20 minutes until the sprouts are losing their bite and the chicory is softened.

5   Leave to cool for a few minutes and then toss with the spring onions, radishes and most of the chives.

6   Divide between plates or place in a nice serving dish, then drizzle the aioli over the warm salad and scatter over the remaining chive batons.

YELLOW COURGETTE, ASPARAGUS & PEA SHOOT SALAD
WITH RED BASIL OIL & CASHEW CREAM

SERVES 4–6

This elegant and simple raw salad is all about letting the natural colours and flavours of summer vegetables shine through. If you can't get yellow courgettes, you can use regular green ones.

1. Using a French-style peeler, slice long thin strips off the courgettes until you reach the seeds, then discard the seedy centre.

2. Remove the tough part of the asparagus by bending each spear at the stalk end and allowing it to snap where the tender part begins. Discard the tough ends (or save them for stock), and cut the tender part into strips as thin as you can manage.

3. Toss the courgette and asparagus strips with the lemon juice and salt in a bowl, cover with clingfilm and leave them to stand in the refrigerator for 30 minutes–1 hour.

4. To make the red basil oil, simply blend all the ingredients in a blender, or in a measuring jug with a stick blender, until smooth.

5. Give the courgettes and asparagus a little squeeze to remove the excess liquid, then toss with the pea shoots and 4 tablespoons of the red basil oil in a large bowl.

6. Put a tablespoon of the cashew cream on each plate and then a small handful of the salad. Drizzle over a little more of the red basil oil to serve.

2–3 yellow courgettes
12 asparagus spears
juice of ½ lemon
⅓ teaspoon sea salt flakes
150g (5½oz) pea shoots
4–6 tablespoons Cashew Cream (*see* page 248), to serve

FOR THE RED BASIL OIL
30g (1oz) red basil, tough stems removed
grated zest and juice of ½ orange
¼ teaspoon agave syrup
100ml (3½fl oz) light olive oil
sea salt flakes

RAW URAB SALAD

Our friend Agung introduced this Balinese fresh coconut and papaya salad to us. Originally from Bali, he is the most amazing cook and uses loads of fabulous ingredients and flavour combinations. Agung's authentic version is mixed with sautéed spinach and doesn't have the papaya pickle, so we hope he won't mind our taking liberties. We thought this was perfect to convert into a raw dish for our summer menu.

Cracking coconuts can be a bit of a performance, but leaving the coconut in a warm place for a while will make the task much easier. After cracking, again leave for a bit to aid the removal of the flesh from the shell. You can find green papaya in Asian shops, but if you can't track it down, use a deseeded cucumber instead.

1   Combine the coriander seeds, chilli, garlic and lime leaves in a mortar and pound to a chunky paste with the pestle. You can also do this with an electric spice grinder or with a stick blender fitted with the chopping/drum attachment.

2   Pierce the 3 eyes of the coconut with a metal skewer and drain out the coconut milk. Place the coconut in a sturdy plastic bag before smashing it on a hard surface outdoors to crack the shell. After leaving the cracked coconut for about 15 minutes (*see* recipe introduction), remove the coconut flesh from the shell, leaving the inner skin on.

3   Grate the coconut on the large-holed side of a box grater.

4   Combine the spice paste with the grated coconut in a bowl. Grate in the palm sugar and mix through thoroughly, crushing it in your hands as you go. You need to massage it for about 5 minutes to really integrate all the flavours. You should notice the coconut changing colour to an orange tone and the texture will soften.

5   To make the pickled vegetables, shred the green papaya, daikon and carrots with a julienne peeler. Add to a glass or ceramic bowl with the remaining pickling ingredients and toss to combine. Cover and leave to stand at room temperature for 30 minutes, or leave overnight in the refrigerator.

6   Combine the coconut with the pickled vegetables. Garnish with coriander leaves and finely sliced spring onions and serve along with the slices of ripe papaya.

SERVES 4

1 tablespoon coriander seeds, coarsely ground
1 small red chilli
2 garlic cloves, peeled
5 fresh kaffir lime leaves, deveined and finely shredded
1 coconut
20g (¾oz) palm sugar
1 large or 2 small ripe papaya, peeled, deseeded and sliced into slim wedges, to serve

FOR THE PICKLED VEGETABLES

1 small green papaya, peeled and deseeded
1 small daikon (mooli), peeled
2 carrots, peeled
200g (7oz) bean sprouts
1 green chilli, finely chopped
20g (¾oz) fresh root ginger, peeled and finely grated
3 tablespoons agave syrup
juice of 6 limes
pinch of turmeric

TO GARNISH

coriander leaves
finely sliced spring onions

POLENTA–DUSTED ARTICHOKE, GREEN BEAN & BROCCOLI FRITO MISTO

A twist on an Italian classic, the addition of polenta in the coating gives these veg a pleasing crunch, and paired with our Roast Garlic Aioli (*see* page 181) they are really moreish. You can use any mix of vegetables you like, bearing in mind that you want them to cook quickly, so choose thin vegetables such as asparagus or soft vegetables like courgette that can be cut up and cooked within 2–3 minutes.

1   Mix the dusting ingredients together in a bowl. Place the yogurt in a separate bowl.

2   In small batches, dip the vegetables in the yogurt, shaking off the excess. Then dust with the polenta mixture, patting it down gently to ensure they are evenly coated.

3   Heat the oil for frying in a large frying pan over a medium heat until it reaches about 180°C (350°F) or until a cube of bread browns in 30 seconds. First, fry the sage leaves for the garnish for a couple of minutes until they are crispy, then drain from the pan on to kitchen paper to absorb the excess oil.

4   Then fry the vegetables, in small batches, for about 2 minutes on each side until they are crispy and golden brown in colour. Drain them from the pan on to kitchen paper as for the sage leaves.

5   Serve hot, garnished with the fried sage leaves, along with lemon wedges and a side of the roast garlic aioli.

SERVES 4

300ml (10fl oz) soya yogurt

8 good-quality artichoke hearts in oil (such as Smokey), drained

100g (3½oz) Tenderstem broccoli stems

50g (1¾oz) green beans

200ml (7fl oz) vegetable oil, for frying

250ml (9fl oz) Roast Garlic Aioli (*see* page 181), to serve

FOR DUSTING

100g (3½oz) gluten-free plain flour

100g (3½oz) fine polenta

good pinch of salt

TO GARNISH

5g (⅛oz) sage leaves

lemon wedges

SERVES 6

300g (10½oz) short-grain brown rice

salt

FOR THE BROTH

splash of sesame oil

1 large white onion, roughly chopped

1 large carrot, peeled and roughly chopped

½ large fennel bulb, roughly sliced

2 spring onions, roughly chopped

4 fresh or dried shiitake mushrooms, roughly sliced

½ sheet of nori seaweed

50g (1¾oz) fresh root ginger, peeled and sliced, plus 20g (¾oz) peeled and very finely sliced for adding at the end

6 garlic cloves, peeled

100g (3½oz) coriander stems (reserve the tops to garnish)

6 fresh kaffir lime leaves, roughly sliced

1 lemon grass stalk

1 green chilli, sliced

2 star anise

4 tablespoons water

4 tablespoons tamari

500ml (18fl oz) apple juice

60g (2¼oz) palm sugar (or raw coconut sugar, or 40g/1½oz light muscovado sugar)

THAI GREEN CONGEE
WITH BROWN RICE

We developed this dish for our Veganuary Menu with the post-holidays detox and health kick in mind. Congee is a breakfast dish found throughout Asia, which is usually made with glutinous white rice to achieve a soft porridge, but we love the nutty texture of this fragrant brown rice version. By all means eat this at breakfast time if you wish, but we see this as a lovely light lunch or dinner dish. The ingredients list for the broth is a little long, but you are essentially making a stock and therefore you can swap most of the vegetables for something similar you need to use up.

The recipe makes a large batch of broth, so you can freeze any extra in zip-seal bags if you want to prepare a smaller quantity of congee by reducing the amount of rice. Equally, we love all the green vegetables piled on top, but you can be selective and use whichever veg you like.

1   For the broth, heat the sesame oil in a large saucepan, add all the vegetables along with the nori, sliced ginger, garlic, herbs, chilli and star anise and sauté over a medium heat, stirring frequently, until they are starting to soften.

2   Add the measured water, tamari, apple juice, sugar and tamarind and bring to the boil, then simmer until the broth has nearly reduced by half, stirring frequently.

3   Remove from the heat and add the lime juice and salt to taste, then leave to cool for 30 minutes before straining.

4   Meanwhile, wash the brown rice thoroughly and then drain. Bring a large saucepan of salted water to the boil, add the rice and bring back to the boil, then cover and simmer until nearly cooked (usually around 20 minutes, but check in relation to the cooking time on the packet). It should still have a fair amount of bite.

5   Drain the rice and add to the broth. Cook, uncovered, for about 20 minutes until the rice has fully cooked and the broth has reduced. Stir in the remaining finely sliced ginger.

>>

6   For the vegetables, heat the blended oil in a wok to a high heat, add all the prepared veg and toss a few times, then add a ladleful of hot broth and cook for a couple of minutes until softened but still crunchy.

7   To serve, place a large cup of rice and broth in each bowl and top with the vegetables. Garnish with the sliced spring onions, the reserved coriander tops and a lime wedge. Serve with a side of seed-weed (toasted seeds and seaweed).

6 tablespoons Asian sweet
   tamarind concentrate
juice of 3 limes
salt

FOR THE VEGETABLES
splash of blended oil (half
   sesame and half sunflower)
6 Tenderstem broccoli stems,
   cut into batons
300g (10½oz) Chinese
   cabbage, sliced
4 pak choi, quartered
100g (3½oz) kale stripped
   of its stems, chopped
100g (3½oz) shiitake
   mushrooms, sliced
100g (3½oz) shelled edamame
   beans
½ fennel bulb, trimmed, cored
   and sliced
1 courgette, finely sliced
6 spring onions, cut into small
   batons, plus extra, sliced,
   to garnish

TO SERVE
lime wedges, to garnish
Seed-weed (see page 121)

BRAZILIAN BLACK BEAN SOUP
WITH RAW CORN SALSA

Black beans, a core ingredient in Brazilian cooking, have such a wonderful rich colour and taste that you don't need to add a huge amount of other ingredients. Victor Passos, one of our Brazilian chefs, says that the bay leaves are key to an authentic Brazilian flavour and they certainly work well here. We've introduced a vibrant raw corn salsa to offset the rich flavour of the beans and add a dash of freshness and colour.

1   To make the soup, heat a big splash of oil in a saucepan, add the onions, chillies and garlic and sauté over a medium heat, stirring frequently, until the onions are translucent.

2   Add the spices and cook over a low heat, stirring, for 1–2 minutes, then add the beans with their liquid, stock and bay leaves to the pan and bring up to a very low simmer.

3   Add the peppers and sweet potato and cook gently, uncovered, for around 45 minutes, stirring occasionally, until the sweet potatoes are cooked but not disintegrating. Remove from the heat while you make the salsa.

4   To make the corn salsa, wash the corn cobs, then cut off the kernels by holding each cob upright with its base on the chopping board and slicing from the top downwards with a sharp knife. Don't cut too close to the cob, as this part can be a bit fibrous. Add the corn kernels to a bowl with the remaining ingredients and mix to combine.

5   Before serving, transfer one-third of the soup (about 200ml/ 7fl oz) to a blender, or to a measuring jug for using a stick blender, and blend until smooth. Return to the pan and mix with the rest of the soup, then reheat, adding a little water to thin if necessary.

6   Serve the soup in bowls with a heaped tablespoon of corn salsa and a lime wedge.

SERVES 4–6

light oil (such as groundnut or sunflower), for sautéeing
2 white onions, finely diced
2 red chillies, finely chopped
5 large garlic cloves, grated or finely chopped
1½ tablespoons smoked paprika
½ tablespoon ground cumin
2 × 400g (14oz) cans black beans
1 litre (1¾ pints) Dark Vegetable Stock (*see* page 251) or French onion stock (from cubes)
5 bay leaves
3 large red peppers, roasted and skinned (*see* page 180), or 5 piquillo peppers from a jar (or other roasted and skinned red peppers), drained
1 small sweet potato, peeled (150g/5½oz prepared weight) and diced into 2cm (¾-inch) pieces
lime wedges, to serve

FOR THE CORN SALSA
2 corn on the cobs, husks and fibres removed
½ red chilli, finely diced
6 spring onions, finely sliced
½ small red onion, finely diced
40g (1½oz) coriander, finely chopped

ROAST JERUSALEM ARTICHOKE & BUTTER BEAN SOUP

I wish I could give you some amazing method of peeling Jerusalem artichokes, but I'm afraid there is no magic trick – just try to choose the least knobbly ones. You can simply wash and scrub them and the flavour of the soup will still be really good, but it will have a darker colour and a less smooth texture. Roasting them really intensifies their amazing flavour, which dominates this soup. The butter beans provide a smooth base to get a really creamy soup without adding cream, and hazelnuts add a lovely crunch, but you can omit them if you wish.

1 Preheat the oven to 200°C (400°F), Gas Mark 6.
2 Rub the Jerusalem artichokes with a little olive oil and sprinkle with salt. Wrap them in baking parchment and then foil, sealing the package tightly. Place on a roasting tray and roast for 1 hour, turning the parcel over halfway through.
3 Heat a splash of olive oil in a large saucepan, add the shallots, garlic and margarine and sauté over a medium heat for 1 minute, stirring. Then add the rosemary and cook until the shallots are translucent and beginning to turn golden, stirring frequently.
4 Add all the remaining ingredients, including the roasted Jerusalem artichokes, and bring up to a gentle simmer. Cook, uncovered, for 20–30 minutes until the beans and artichokes are breaking down.
5 Meanwhile, spread the hazelnuts out on a baking tray and roast in the oven for 10–15 minutes. Remove from the oven. If they have skins, tip them on to a clean tea towel, bunch the tea towel around the nuts to form a sack and massage them to rub the skins off. Open the tea towel and carefully pick out the nuts (some will still have some skin left on them, but that's OK). Crush the nuts to fine crumbs by pulsing in a food processor, by using a stick blender fitted with the chopping/drum attachment or by crushing in a bowl with the end of a rolling pin.
6 Transfer the soup to a blender, or use a stick blender, and blend until completely smooth.
7 Reheat the soup if necessary and serve with a scattering of hazelnuts, a dash of either lemon-infused olive oil or hazelnut oil and fried sage leaves sprinkled with the sea salt flakes.

SERVES 6–8 AS A STARTER OR 4–6 AS A MAIN

1kg (2lb 4oz) Jerusalem artichokes, peeled (don't worry if there are a few bits of skin left on)
olive oil
4 shallots, sliced
5–7 garlic cloves, chopped or grated
1 tablespoon vegan margarine
1 sprig of rosemary, leaves picked and chopped
400g (14oz) can butter beans, rinsed and drained
1 litre (1¾ pints) Light Vegetable Stock (*see* page 251)
350ml (12fl oz) dry white wine
salt

TO SERVE
150g (5½oz) whole hazelnuts
lemon-infused olive oil or hazelnut oil
fried sage leaves (*see* page 66)
¼ teaspoon sea salt flakes

OGÓRKI SOUP

SERVES 4-6

splash of light oil (such as
groundnut or sunflower)

1 onion, quartered

1 large carrot, peeled and
roughly chopped

1 celery stick, roughly chopped

¼ fennel bulb, roughly
chopped

2.5 litres (4½ pints) Light
Vegetable Stock (see page
251) or 2.5 litres (4½ pints)
water with 3 light vegetable
stock cubes dissolved in it

2 parsley stems or green
leek tops

2 bay leaves

2 whole allspice berries

300g (10½oz) waxy potatoes
(such as Rooster)

200g (7oz) Sour Dill Pickles
(see page 192), diced

50ml (2fl oz) pickling juice
from the Sour Dill Pickles,
plus extra to taste (optional)

2 pinches of ground white
pepper

salt

TO GARNISH

25g (1oz) dill, chopped

soya cream (optional)

A Polish classic, the distinctive flavour of this soup comes from sour pickles or *ogórki kiszone*, also known as dill pickles or haimisha pickles. To some people the idea of making a soup with pickles might seem a little odd, but if you think of the sour savoury tang of a caper but milder, it begins to make more sense.

The best sour pickles are homemade and are quite easy to prepare (*see* page 192), but if you don't have the time, use your favourite sour gherkins - the best shop-bought gherkins are those that contain no preservatives and haven't been pasteurized.

This soup is all about the broth, and a tasty light-coloured broth is needed here, so follow the recipe for Light Stock on page 251. But if using stock cubes, make sure you opt for a vegetable stock that is light in colour, otherwise the soup will look muddy and won't be as attractive when serving.

1   Heat the oil in a large saucepan, add the onion, carrot, celery and fennel and sauté over a medium heat for 6-8 minutes, stirring frequently and trying not to give them much colour. Add the stock, parsley stems or leek tops, bay leaves and allspice and bring to a simmer, then cook for about 20-25 minutes until the stock has reduced by a quarter.

2   While the stock is reducing, peel the potatoes and cut into bite-sized chunks. Wash in plenty of cold water and drain, then put them in a saucepan with enough water to cover and a little salt. Bring to the boil and then cover and simmer for 15-20 minutes until they are fully cooked. Drain in a colander and leave to air-dry.

3   Once the stock has reduced enough, strain and return to the pan over the heat. Taste to see if it has enough flavour, and if necessary, return to a simmer and reduce the stock further until it has intensified in flavour. Add the diced sour dill pickles and pickling juice, potatoes and white pepper and simmer for a further 8-10 minutes, then taste and adjust the seasoning if necessary.

4   Depending on the strength of the pickling juice and on your taste, you can add more juice for a more sour soup.

5   Serve garnished with the chopped dill and a touch of soya cream if you like.

GINGER SPRING VEGETABLE & NOODLE BROTH

Fragrant and mild flavoured, this broth lends itself to the sweet taste of baby spring vegetables. That being said, you can make this at any time of the year and top with seasonal vegetables of your choice. I always make the broth in largish batches because of the long boiling time involved, wanting to get a good return on my time investment by having extra to keep for future use. So if you're cooking for fewer people, just reduce the topping vegetables and store the leftover broth in zip-seal bags in the freezer. That way, you will have a healthy delicious meal ready in minutes.

I like to use fat udon noodles, which come in packs divided into separate portions, but you can use any noodles you prefer. Most Asian noodles are designed to be cooked directly in broth or soup, but check the cooking instructions on the pack.

1   For the broth, heat the oil in a large saucepan, add all the broth ingredients except the measured water, noodles and watercress and cook for 5 minutes until beginning to soften.

2   Add the measured water and bring to the boil, then simmer until the broth has reduced by half, stirring frequently.

3   Remove from the heat and strain. Return to the pan and add the remaining very finely sliced ginger. Bring up to the boil, stir in the noodles and cook according to the packet instructions.

4   While the noodles are cooking, for the vegetables, heat the blended oil in a wok to a high heat, add all the prepared veg and toss a few times, then add a ladleful of hot broth and cook for a couple of minutes until the vegetables are softened but still crunchy.

5   Ladle the broth and noodles into large bowls and top with the stir-fried vegetables and a few sprigs of watercress.

SERVES 6

FOR THE BROTH
3 tablespoons sesame oil or light oil (such as groundnut or sunflower)
100g (3½oz) fresh root ginger, peeled and sliced, plus 20g (¾oz), peeled and very finely sliced for adding at the end
½ fennel bulb, roughly sliced
5 garlic cloves, peeled
5 star anise
5 fresh or dried shiitake mushrooms, roughly sliced
1 white onion, roughly sliced
5 spring onions, chopped
100ml (3½fl oz) mirin
pinch of ground white pepper
1 sheet of nori seaweed
2 litres (3½ pints) water
100g (3½oz) udon noodles per person
handful of watercress, to garnish

FOR THE VEGETABLES
glug of blended oil (half sesame and half sunflower)
3 pak choi, quartered
6 baby carrots, scrubbed and halved
4 baby fennel bulbs, sliced
6 baby leeks
½ white onion, sliced
5 spring onions, cut into 5cm (2-inch) batons

MAINS & BBQ

ROMANO PEPPERS
FILLED WITH DIRTY FREEKEH, TOBACCO ONIONS & SPICED TAHINI SAUCE

Romano peppers are the long, pointed peppers that are sometimes called sweet peppers, with much thinner skins and far fewer seeds than their better-known cousins. Perfect for roasting, the skins can be easily removed if you wish, but can also be left on, as they perfectly fine to eat.

The freekeh filling is based on the more familiar dirty rice, which is a signature dish of Lebanon. While not spicy hot, it is nevertheless heavily spiced, so if you prefer a milder dish, just halve the quantity of spice mix. We've provided a recipe for Baharat Spice Mix (*see* page 194), which is based on Lebanese seven spice, a mix that you can readily buy ready prepared. We serve this dish with Sautéed Spinach (*see* page 34).

1   Preheat the oven to 190°C (375°F), Gas Mark 5.
2   Wash the peppers and then, using a sharp knife, make a slit about two-thirds down the length of each pepper. Rub with olive oil and then scatter with baharat or Lebanese seven spice mix and a little salt on a baking tray.
3   Roast the peppers for 10-15 minutes until they begin to soften. They should be soft enough to open, but not fully cooked. Remove from the oven and leave to cool slightly. Leave the oven on.
4   While the peppers are cooking, begin making the dirty freekeh. Put the Puy lentils in a small saucepan, cover well with water and simmer over a medium heat for 20-25 minutes until just cooked but still firm. Drain and set aside.
5   Heat the oil in a saucepan, add the onion, garlic and chilli and sauté over a medium heat for a few minutes, stirring frequently, until the onion is translucent. Add the spices and cook over a low heat for a couple of minutes, stirring, until they release their aroma.
6   Add the freekeh and cook for a couple of minutes, stirring, until lightly toasted. Add the lentils and cover with water, then stir in the orange zest and juice. Bring to the boil, then cover and simmer over a low heat for 15 minutes.
7   Turn off the heat and leave to sit, covered, for 10 minutes. Stir in the remaining dirty freekeh ingredients and season to taste.
8   Open up the peppers a little and scoop out the seeds. Don't worry about getting them all out and be careful not to tear the peppers.

>>

SERVES 6

6 large or 10 small Romano
   peppers
olive oil, for rubbing
Baharat Spice Mix (*see* page
   194) or shop-bought
   Lebanese seven spice mix,
   for scattering
salt

FOR THE DIRTY FREEKEH
100g (3½oz) Puy lentils
splash of light olive oil
1 small white onion, finely diced
2 garlic cloves, finely chopped
   or grated
1 small red chilli, finely
   chopped
1 tablespoon Baharat Spice
   Mix (*see* page 194) or
   shop-bought Lebanese
   seven spice mix
1 teaspoon turmeric
90g (3¼oz) freekeh
grated zest and juice of 1 orange
20g (¾oz) pine nuts, toasted
20g (¾oz) currants
20g (¾oz) ready-to-eat dried
   apricots, finely chopped
½ tablespoon soft dark
   brown sugar
20g (¾oz) flat leaf parsley,
   leaves picked and chopped
salt and pepper

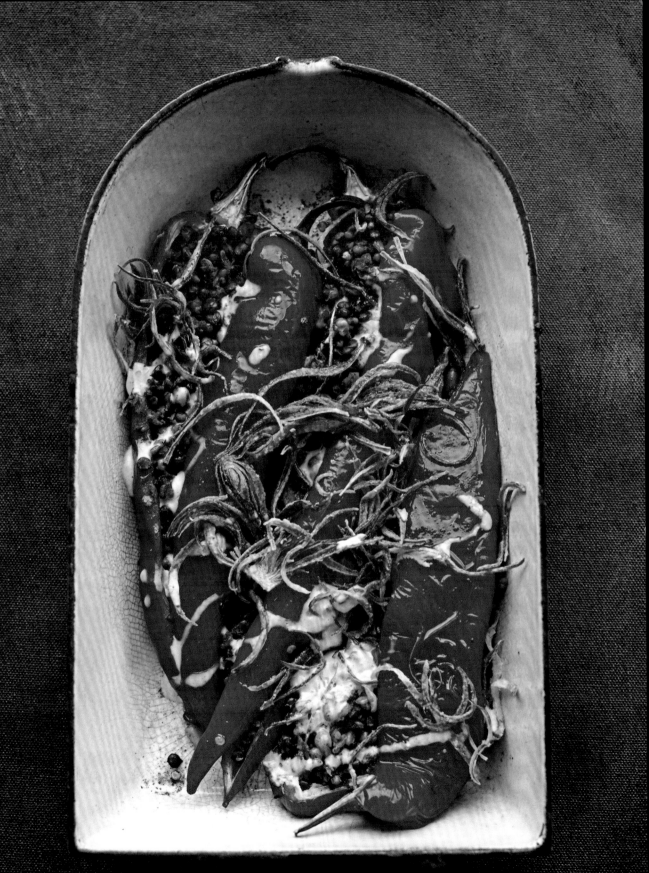

9 Fill each pepper with the freekeh mixture and then pack the peppers into a baking dish quite tightly. Bake for 15–20 minutes until they begin to soften.

10 To make the spiced tahini sauce, using a small balloon whisk, whisk all the ingredients together in a bowl to combine, then leave to cool. If the sauce thickens too much, add more water and whisk well to combine. It should be a pouring consistency.

11 For the tobacco onions, season the cornflour or rice flour with salt and pepper, then toss the onion in the flour until just coated. Heat about 1cm (½ inch) light oil in a large saucepan or frying pan to a medium heat. Add the onion and fry for 3–4 minutes until dark golden brown and crunchy. Drain from the pan on to kitchen paper to absorb the excess oil.

12 Serve the stuffed peppers with the tobacco onions and a drizzle of spiced tahini sauce.

FOR THE SPICED TAHINI SAUCE
200ml (7fl oz) tahini
2½ tablespoons agave syrup
½ tablespoon Baharat Spice Mix (*see* page 194) or
1 teaspoon ground cumin
200ml (7fl oz) warm water
juice of 2 lemons
salt

FOR THE TOBACCO ONIONS
2–3 tablespoons cornflour or rice flour
1 white onion, very finely sliced
light oil (such as groundnut or sunflower), for frying
salt and pepper

SMOKED TOFU & WHITE BEAN SAUSAGES

MAKES 8-10 SAUSAGES; SERVES 4-5

1 fennel bulb, cored and finely diced (including the stalks)

1 onion, finely diced

2 large garlic cloves, finely diced

3 tablespoons light olive oil for roasting, plus 1½ tablespoons for the sausage mix

½ tablespoon fennel seeds

325g (11½oz) pack Chinese-style fresh firm tofu, diced

100g (3½oz) smoked tofu, diced

400g (14oz) can white beans (such as cannellini, haricot or butter beans), drained and rinsed

120g (4¼oz) Sausage and Burger Base Mix (see page 249)

350g (12oz) dessert apples, grated

20g (¾oz) gram flour

20g (¾oz) chives, chopped

1 teaspoon salt

½ teaspoon ground black pepper

100ml (3½fl oz) vegetable oil, for frying

TO SERVE
Creamy Mustard Mash (see page 164)

Sautéed Spinach (see page 34)

Cider Jus (see page 250)

A staple every year on our winter menu, these white bean, smoked tofu, apple and fennel sausages are light and fresh (see photograph overleaf). Served with fluffy mashed potatoes, sautéed spinach and our pear Cider Jus (see page 250), this is perfect food for picking you up during the colder months.

The firm tofu must be Chinese-style fresh tofu, and the best place to buy fresh tofu will be your local Asian supermarket. The Clean Bean brand made in London will work well. Unfortunately, any other tofu won't work for this recipe.

1 Preheat the oven to 200°C (400°F), Gas Mark 6.

2 Toss the diced fennel, onion and garlic in the 3 tablespoons light olive oil along with the fennel seeds in a bowl, then spread out on a baking tray and roast for 15-20 minutes until fully cooked. Remove from the oven and leave to cool. Leave the oven on.

3 Using your hands, crumble the tofu to a paste into a large bowl and mix with all the remaining ingredients, including the remaining 1½ tablespoons light olive oil (but excluding the vegetable oil). Transfer the mixture to a food processor and give it a quick pulse for 30 seconds to bring it together.

4 Heat up a frying pan with a little of the vegetable oil over a medium heat and fry off a small portion of the sausage mixture, then taste for seasoning and adjust if necessary.

5 Roll the remaining mixture into small sausages about 8cm (3½ inches) long. Add all the remaining oil to the pan and heat, then fry the sausages over a medium heat for 6-8 minutes, turning them frequently, until they are golden brown. Transfer to a baking tray and finish cooking in the oven for 10-15 minutes.

6 Serve with the mashed potatoes, sautéed spinach and cider jus.

SPICED SEITAN BALLS
WITH CHICKPEAS & BLACK KALE

The seasoning of these seitan balls is fragrant and Middle Eastern inspired rather than the classic *polpette*, or Italian meatball, flavours. As such, they pair well with our Spiced Tahini Sauce (*see* page 80), and can be served with basmati rice or flatbread if you're looking for a more filling meal.

1   Dice the seitan into small cubes and add to a food processor, then pulse until finely minced.

2   Heat a splash of oil in a frying pan, add the onions and sauté over a medium heat for a few minutes, stirring frequently, until they begin to colour. Add the garlic and cook for a further couple of minutes. Add all the spices and dried mint along with the seitan and cook for a few minutes, stirring, until the spices release their aroma. Leave to cool.

3   Tip the cooled mixture into a bowl, add the flour, breadcrumbs and suet and mix together well, adding a few tablespoons of water to help bring it together. You should be able to form the mixture into balls that hold their shape. Divide and roll the mixture into about 24 small balls, then set aside.

4   Preheat the oven to 190°C (375°F), Gas Mark 5.

5   Heat a frying pan with a good splash of oil, add the seitan balls and lightly fry over a medium heat for 6-7 minutes, turning frequently, until they begin to colour. Transfer to a baking tray and place in the oven while you prepare the black kale and chickpeas.

6   For the kale and chickpeas, using the same frying pan, drain off any excess oil and return to the heat. Add the kale and sauté over a medium-high heat for 2 minutes, stirring, until it begins to wilt slightly. Stir in the chickpeas, coriander and salt and cook for a further few minutes to heat the chickpeas through.

7   Serve the kale and chickpeas with the seitan balls, drizzled with a little extra virgin olive oil, with a lemon wedge on the side.

MAKES ABOUT 24 BALLS; SERVES 4

400g (14oz) seitan

light oil (such as groundnut, sunflower or light olive oil), for sautéeing and frying

2 onions (200g/7oz), diced

4 garlic cloves, crushed

3 teaspoons ground coriander

3 teaspoons sweet paprika

¼ teaspoon cracked black pepper

2 teaspoons dried mint

5 tablespoons plain flour

150g (5½oz) fresh white breadcrumbs

3 tablespoons vegetarian suet

FOR THE BLACK KALE AND CHICKPEAS

200g (7oz) cavolo nero (black kale), washed, stripped of its stems and roughly chopped

400g (14oz) can chickpeas, drained and rinsed

1 teaspoon ground coriander

½ teaspoon salt

TO SERVE

50ml (2fl oz) extra virgin olive oil

lemon wedges

AUBERGINE CURRY

SERVES 4-6

4 large aubergines (850g/
   1lb 14oz total weight)

100ml (3½fl oz) light oil (such
   as groundnut or sunflower),
   plus an extra splash

¼ teaspoon black mustard
   seeds

10-12 dried curry leaves

4 tablespoons dried mung dahl

1 onion, finely sliced

2 teaspoons ground coriander

2 teaspoons cumin seeds

1 teaspoon fenugreek seeds

1 teaspoon turmeric

½ teaspoon chilli powder

7 plum tomatoes (600g/
   1lb 5oz total weight), cored
   and quartered

3 tablespoons tomato purée

1 teaspoon salt

1 tablespoon caster sugar

600ml (20fl oz) water

TO SERVE

Cardamom and Pea Basmati
   Rice (see page 131)

Coconut Chutney (see page
   132)

They say that the English love a good curry, and this certainly rings true at Mildreds, with curry having been a staple on the menu since 1988. This recipe is from our archives, devised by a previous head chef, Gillian Snowball; a great quick, easy curry bursting with flavour, which was on our menu for years and enjoyed by many. It's great served with our Cardamom and Pea Basmati Rice (see page 131) and Coconut Chutney (see page 132). Coriander Naan (see page 131) is another great option for those who can eat gluten.

1   Preheat the oven to 200°C (400°F), Gas Mark 6.

2   Cut the aubergine into quarters, then into large chunks about 6cm (2½ inches) in size. Place on a baking tray, drizzle with the 100ml (3½fl oz) light oil and toss well, making sure the aubergine pieces are evenly coated. Roast for 15-20 minutes until fully cooked and coloured.

3   While the aubergines are roasting, heat a splash of light oil in a large saucepan, add the black mustard seeds and cook over a low heat for a few minutes until they begin to pop. Add the curry leaves and dahl and cook over a medium heat, stirring occasionally, for a couple of minutes until the dahl turns light brown. Then add the onion and sweat over a low heat for about 10 minutes until it begins to soften.

4   Add all the spices and cook gently for 2-3 minutes, stirring, until they release their aroma, being careful not to let them burn. Add three-quarters of the tomatoes, the tomato purée, salt, sugar and measured water, bring to a simmer over a medium heat and cook for 15-20 minutes, stirring frequently, until the sauce thickens slightly and the tomatoes have broken down completely.

5   Add the remaining tomatoes and the roasted aubergines and cook for a further 10-12 minutes until the tomatoes are fully cooked but still holding their shape.

6   Serve with the basmati rice and chutney.

"CHICKEN" & WAFFLES

This is a classic soul food dish for which you can use your favourite vegan substitute for chicken. Vegan "chicken" has become a regular feature at some of the coolest meat-free pop-up kitchens and cafés. It is usually made from textured soya protein, but our preference is to use lightly flavoured seitan. For extra crunch, we dust our vegan "chicken" with a lightly spiced golden coating made from polenta.

Served with our Rainbow Root Slaw (*see* page 140), the mix of sweet and savoury along with a subtle kick from the spices in the vegan "chicken" makes this comfort eating at its best!

1   Heat the vegetable oil for frying in a frying pan to about 180°C (350°F) or until a cube of bread browns in 30 seconds.

2   While the oil is heating up, mix all the ingredients for dusting together in a bowl. Place the yogurt in a separate bowl.

3   Dip each vegan "chicken" piece in the yogurt and then shake off any excess. Cover with the dusting mixture, patting it down gently to make sure the entire piece is well coated, then add to the hot oil in the pan slowly and gently so that it begins to crisp up and doesn't stick to the base of the pan. Fry the coated "chicken", in batches, for 2-3 minutes on each side until deep golden brown and crispy - be careful not to overcrowd the pan, as this will reduce the temperature of the oil and the coating won't be crispy. Drain on to kitchen paper to absorb the excess oil.

4   Serve the crispy "chicken" on top of the waffles with the slaw and a drizzle of maple syrup.

SERVES 4

200ml (7fl oz) vegetable oil, for frying
300ml (10fl oz) soya yogurt
300g (10½oz) vegan "chicken" pieces (defrosted if frozen)

FOR DUSTING
½ teaspoon smoked paprika
1½ teaspoons sweet paprika
¼ teaspoon cayenne pepper
¼ teaspoon dried thyme or oregano
½ teaspoon onion or celery salt
2 teaspoons garlic powder
100g (3½oz) plain flour
200g (7oz) fine polenta

TO SERVE
4 Porridge Waffles (*see* page 19)
300g (10½oz) Rainbow Root Slaw (*see* page 140)
100ml (3½fl oz) maple syrup

DRUNKEN TEMPURA–BATTERED SILKEN TOFU
WITH WASABI PEAS & EDAMAME

Silken tofu, as the names suggests, is a beautifully smooth Japanese tofu. You will generally find it vacuum packed; because it's very delicate, remove it carefully from the pack and slice with a sharp knife.

The quantity of wasabi you add to the peas will depend on your taste and the brand of wasabi you are using, as they vary hugely in strength, but the quantity specified in this recipe gives quite a mild result, though you can omit it altogether if you prefer. We would serve this with a cup of steamed jasmine rice for a filling main, or pair it with some soba noodles and Japanese pickles (*see* Simple Pickled Daikon, page 119) for a summer twist and serve the peas cold, along with an ice-cold gluten-free beer.

1. First make the marinade and dip. Put the mirin, lemon juice, ginger, wakame and measured water in a small saucepan and bring to a gentle simmer, stirring. Cook for a few minutes, then remove from the heat and strain into a bowl.

2. Place the tofu pieces in a dish and pour over a couple of tablespoons of the marinade. Cover with clingfilm and leave to marinate at room temperature while you prepare the other components.

3. Add the sweet chilli sauce, tamari and chilli to the remaining marinade and stir well for the dip.

4. Next make the wasabi peas. Heat the sesame oil in a medium-sized saucepan, add the garlic and chilli and fry over a medium heat for 1–2 minutes, stirring, until the garlic is just beginning to brown.

5. Add the peas or petit pois and fry for 1 minute, stirring, then add the measured water and sugar and simmer for 4–5 minutes. Remove from the heat and add the coriander.

6. Transfer the pea mixture to a food processor, or use a stick blender, and blend to a slightly chunky purée. Return the peas to the heat and add the edamame, soya cream and enough wasabi paste to give the peas a bit of a kick, or to your taste.

7. To prepare the tofu to fry, cut the nori sheets into 3 strips to make 6 strips in total. Carefully remove the tofu pieces from the marinade and pat dry with kitchen paper. Wrap each tofu piece in a nori strip.

>>

SERVES 4–6

300g (10½oz) pack silken tofu, cut widthways into 6 slices
2 sheets of nori seaweed
600ml (20fl oz) light oil (such as groundnut or sunflower), for deep-frying
steamed or boiled rice, to serve (optional)

FOR THE MARINADE AND DIP
200ml (7fl oz) mirin
3 tablespoons lemon juice
15g (½oz) peeled fresh root ginger, thinly sliced or grated
1 teaspoon dried wakame seaweed
200ml (7fl oz) water
50ml (2fl oz) sweet chilli sauce
50ml (2fl oz) tamari
1 red chilli, chopped

FOR THE WASABI PEAS
2–3 tablespoons sesame oil
2 garlic cloves, finely chopped
¼ red chilli, chopped
350g (12oz) peas or petit pois
200ml (7fl oz) water
½ teaspoon sugar
5 sprigs of coriander, leaves picked and chopped
150g (5½oz) shelled edamame beans
3 tablespoons soya cream
about 2 tablespoons wasabi paste, or to taste

FOR THE BEER BATTER

170g (6oz) gluten-free plain
    flour, plus extra for dusting
    the tofu

1 teaspoon sugar

½ teaspoon gluten-free
    baking powder

½ teaspoon gluten-free
    bicarbonate of soda

330ml (11½fl oz) bottle light
    gluten-free beer

salt

8 Measure out all the batter ingredients, except the beer, into a bowl and then whisk together with a balloon whisk. Dust each piece of wrapped tofu in flour and set aside.

9 Heat the oil for deep-frying in a deep-fryer or a large saucepan to about 180°C (350°F) or until a drop of batter instantly sizzles and cooks when added to the hot oil.

10 Whisk the beer into the dry batter mixture until just combined. Dip 2 or 3 pieces of tofu (depending on the size of your pan) into the batter, one at a time, carefully drop into the oil and deep-fry for a few minutes on each side until they begin to turn golden brown, turning with a slotted spoon. When evenly cooked, scoop out the tofu and place on a wire rack. Be careful not to crowd the pan with tofu, as this will reduce the temperature of the oil and the batter won't be crispy.

11 Serve hot with the dip and wasabi peas on the side, and also, if you wish, some steamed or boiled rice - we like brown jasmine but sushi rice or short-grain are also nice.

FUL MEDAMES
WITH ISRAELI SALAD & DUKKAH

Thought to have originated in Ancient Egypt, ful can be found across North Africa and the Middle East – it's like a very thick, rich soup, similar to dahl, made with dried and then rehydrated whole broad beans (with the skins left on). It is typically eaten for breakfast with warm flatbread and pickles or salad, but we recommend having it for brunch, lunch or dinner.

Ful has hundreds of variations and can be made plain, with just a little cumin, lemon juice and olive oil, or flavoured with chilli and tomatoes or tahini and any number of spices. We prefer a fresher take with chickpeas and fresh tomato, served with a colourful salad. If you want to stretch this to a full feast, serve it with hummus or tahini sauce, pickles and basmati rice.

You will find canned broad beans (also called ful or fava beans) in any shop with a Middle Eastern section. Bear in mind that processed dried broad beans are brown, not pale green. If you can't find canned beans, use dried – wash and soak them in cold water overnight, then simmer gently in unsalted fresh water for an hour until soft, making sure you retain the cooking water. For a gluten-free option, serve without the flatbread or pitta.

1   To make the salad, put half the onion, tomatoes, parsley, mint and lemon juice in a bowl, reserving the rest for the ful. Add all the cucumber and spring onions to the bowl, the sumac, a slug of light olive oil and salt to taste. Toss together well and set aside.

2   For the ful, heat a dry medium-sized saucepan over a gentle heat, add the cumin seeds and toast for a couple of minutes, stirring, until they release their aroma. Remove from the heat and then grind the cumin with a pestle and mortar or an electric spice grinder.

3   Don't wash the pan, just add another glug of light olive oil and return to the heat. Add the reserved onion along with the garlic and chilli and sauté over a medium heat for 5-6 minutes, stirring frequently, until the onion is translucent. Add the sugar, ground cumin, coriander and paprika and cook, stirring, for 2-3 minutes.

>>

SERVES 4-6

I white onion, very finely diced

4 ripe plum or vine tomatoes, cored and diced (including seeds)

80g (3oz) flat leaf parsley, chopped, plus extra to garnish

4 sprigs of mint, leaves picked and chopped

juice of 1 large lemon (or 2 small)

½ cucumber, diced

4 spring onions, finely sliced

large pinch of sumac

light olive oil

1 tablespoon cumin seeds

3–4 garlic cloves, grated or finely chopped

½ red chilli, chopped

pinch of soft light brown sugar

½ teaspoon ground coriander

¼ teaspoon sweet paprika

400g (14oz) can broad beans (ful or fava beans)

400g (14oz) can chickpeas

2 bay leaves

100–200ml (3½–7fl oz) water

salt

olive oil

warm flatbread or pitta
  bread

lemon wedges

6 tablespoons Hazelnut
  and Almond Dukkah
  (*see* page 196)

4   Pour in the canned broad beans and chickpeas with their liquid and bring up to a simmer. Add the reserved tomatoes with the bay leaves and cook gently for 30-45 minutes until thick and creamy, topping up with the measured water as needed when the mixture becomes too thick. Stir the ful frequently during cooking – as with dahl, the success of the dish is in the stirring, which makes the texture creamier.

5   Remove the pan from the heat and add the reserved lemon juice, parsley and mint. Using a stick blender, blend about half the ful to make the mixture slightly smoother but still very chunky with lots of whole beans.

6   Garnish the ful with chopped parsley and serve with the salad, olive oil and warm flatbread or pitta bread, with lemon wedges and the dukkah on the side.

PERSIAN LIME & CHICKPEA STEW

A truly satisfying stew that has a great depth of Persian flavours in all their fragrant sweet and spicy glory. Persian limes are small dried limes used in slow-cooked dishes from the region now known as Iran, and are available from most Middle Eastern supermarkets and online. Fragrant and intensely sour, they can be likened to a more pungent-tasting preserved lemon. You need to make incisions in the limes for them to scent the stew, but we wouldn't recommend you popping them into your mouth whole.

We suggest serving this with simple roast or grilled chard or Sautéed Spinach (see page 34), but you could turn it into a centrepiece for a special meal by serving it with our Grilled Rainbow Chard (see page 148) and warm grilled flatbread (omit this last for a gluten-free option).

1   Preheat the oven to 180°C (350°F), Gas Mark 4.
2   Heat a dry large flameproof casserole dish or saucepan, add the fennel and cumin seeds and gently toast for a couple of minutes, stirring, until they release their aroma. Remove from the heat and then grind the spices with a pestle and mortar or an electric spice grinder.
3   Don't wash the pan, but just add the oil to it and return to the heat, then add the shallots and chilli and sauté over a medium heat for 5–6 minutes, stirring frequently, until the shallots begin to turn golden. Add the ground fennel and cumin with the coriander and turmeric and cook, stirring, for 1–2 minutes.
4   Add the tomatoes, tomato purée, limes, sugar and stock and bring up to a simmer. Add the new potatoes, baby carrots, chickpeas, harissa and salt and warm through for 8–10 minutes before covering and transferring to the oven. If you're using a saucepan, you will need to transfer the stew to an ovenproof baking dish and cover with foil.
5   Bake for 45 minutes–1 hour until the potatoes are fully cooked and the sauce has thickened.
6   Garnish the stew with the chopped parsley and serve with some freshly cooked greens and flatbread.

SERVES 4–6

½ tablespoon fennel seeds
½ tablespoon cumin seeds
glug of light olive oil
2 shallots, sliced
1 small red chilli, chopped
½ tablespoon ground coriander
½ teaspoon turmeric
400g (14oz) can chopped
   tomatoes
1½ tablespoons tomato purée
3 Persian limes, with several
   incisions cut into them
1 tablespoon soft light
   brown sugar
500ml (18fl oz) Dark Vegetable
   Stock (see page 251)
400g (14oz) new potatoes,
   peeled but kept whole
120g (4¼oz) baby carrots,
   topped and, if they are on
   the large side, halved
400g (14oz) can good-quality
   chickpeas, drained and rinsed
1½ tablespoons Persian Lime
   and Rose Harissa (see page
   187) or 1 tablespoon harissa
   mixed with 1 tablespoon dried
   rose petals
salt, to taste
handful of chopped flat leaf
   parsley leaves, to garnish

TO SERVE
cooked chard, spinach or kale
warm grilled flatbread

BEETROOT & FENNEL STEW

This Polish-inspired stew is a recipe that was developed with help from one of our talented head chefs, Marcelo Navarro. It goes well with Polish Potato Dumplings (*see* recipe opposite and photograph overleaf) or you can serve it with a simple side dish of mashed potatoes garnished with freshly chopped dill.

1 Preheat the oven to 200°C (400°F), Gas Mark 6.

2 Trim the fennel, then cut into small wedges, leaving the core in so that they hold together. Place on a baking tray along with the fennel seeds and a splash of oil and toss well to make sure the fennel is evenly coated with oil. Bake for 15-20 minutes until the fennel is cooked and slightly coloured.

3 While the fennel is cooking, heat a large saucepan with a splash of oil, add the onions and fry over a medium heat for a few minutes, stirring frequently, until they have begun to soften. Add the garlic and cook for a couple of minutes, stirring, then add the spices and thyme and cook over a gentle heat for another couple of minutes, stirring, until they release their aroma.

4 Add the apple juice, measured water, tomato purée, passata or blended chopped tomatoes, beetroot, stock cubes, sugar and salt, stir well and bring to a simmer. Reduce the heat and cook for 30 minutes until the beetroot is fully cooked and the sauce has thickened, stirring occasionally to make sure the sauce doesn't catch on the base of the pan.

5 Add the roasted fennel and cook for a further 10-15 minutes.

6 Combine the chopped dill with the soya yogurt in a small bowl and season with the salt. Serve with the stew for spooning on top.

SERVES 4-5

2 fennel bulbs (about 400g/14oz)
½ teaspoon fennel seeds
light olive oil
2 red onions, sliced
3 garlic cloves, crushed
⅛ teaspoon cayenne pepper
1 teaspoon ground allspice
1 tablespoon sweet paprika
2 teaspoons chopped thyme leaves
200ml (7fl oz) apple juice
600ml (20fl oz) water
2 tablespoons tomato purée
400g (14oz) can passata or chopped tomatoes, blended until smooth
700g (1lb 9oz) beetroot, peeled and cut into wedges
2 French onion or vegetable stock cubes, crumbled
½ teaspoon sugar
½ teaspoon salt

TO SERVE
25g (1oz) dill, chopped
200ml (7fl oz) soya yogurt
pinch of salt

POLISH POTATO DUMPLINGS

SERVES 4

550g (1lb 4oz) waxy potatoes
(such as Rooster), peeled
and quartered

60g (2¼oz) potato flour

salt

10g (¼oz) dill, chopped,
to garnish

TO SERVE

Beetroot and Fennel Stew
(see opposite)

cooked chard

This recipe was given to us by Maria Ochendzan. Called *kluski śląskie* in Polish, these dumplings are similar to gnocchi but are smoother and very light. They are great served with Beetroot and Fennel Stew (*see* recipe opposite and photograph overleaf).

Uncooked dumplings cook well from frozen, so double up on the recipe and open freeze the extra batch on a flat tray before bagging them up so that they don't stick together.

1   Put the potatoes in a saucepan with enough water to cover and a little salt. Bring to the boil, cover and simmer for 20 minutes or until tender. Drain in a colander and leave to air-dry for a few minutes.

2   Use a ricer to mash the potatoes. Alternatively, use a wooden spoon to push the potatoes through a fine-mesh sieve. Leave to cool to room temperature in a bowl.

3   Add the potato flour and ½ teaspoon salt to the potato and knead the mixture well for a few minutes until it holds together.

4   Divide the mixture into quarters and roll each quarter out into a log about 3cm (1¼ inch) in diameter. Cut each log into pieces about 2.5cm (1 inch) thick, then roll each piece in between the palms of your hands to form a smooth ball. Press your index finger or thumb into each ball to make an indent. If the mixture doesn't hold together well and is a little dry, add a small splash of water, knead together well and reshape. Cover the dumplings and refrigerate for 20 minutes to set (this helps them to keep their shape when you cook them).

5   To cook the dumplings, fill a large wide saucepan with water and bring to the boil. Drop the dumplings into the pan, a few at a time, making sure the water continues to boil gently and the dumplings are kept moving. Once the dumplings begin to float to the surface, after 1–2 minutes, cook them for a further 2 minutes. (If cooking from frozen, the same rules apply, but be aware that the water temperature will drop more quickly when you add the dumplings - be sure to keep the dumplings moving about on a gentle boil, or they may begin to fall apart while cooking.)

6   Using a slotted spoon, remove the dumplings from the pan and garnish with the chopped dill. Serve immediately with beetroot and fennel stew and some cooked chard.

MALAYSIAN RED CURRY
WITH TOASTED MACADAMIA NUTS & MANGO

We called upon one of our long-serving, accomplished head chefs, Nasralla Soliman, to help devise this dish, using macadamia nuts in much the same way that candle nut is used in Malaysian food, to thicken it and make it extra creamy. But unlike candle nuts, macadamias can be enjoyed toasted on top too. Most food from Thailand, Vietnam, Malaysia and Indonesia gains a lot of its flavour from fish sauces and shrimp paste, so we've used miso here to imitate the fermented salty quality of those ingredients. Galangal is a key ingredient in South Asian cooking, and although it looks very similar to its cousin ginger, its flavour is unique - equally spicy as ginger yet with an earthy pine-like quality, but not to be used with abandon, since it's more strongly flavoured. It's becoming more widely available in supermarkets, but if you can't get it, just substitute ginger.

Making your own curry paste can seem like a lot of work, but it really will give you an edge, because when it comes to depth of flavour, there is no substitute for freshly toasted and ground spices. Having said that, if you like the idea of this curry but don't have the time, we would recommend using a good-quality vegan Thai red curry paste instead, as there are a lot of similarities between Thai and Malaysian cooking. Spice paste keeps very well in the freezer, so if you are making it, consider doubling up and keeping a batch for a quick curry another day.

1 First toast the macadamia nuts. Preheat the oven to 170°C (340°F), Gas Mark 3½. Spread the nuts out on a baking tray and toast for 5 minutes. Remove from the oven and grind them coarsely, either by pulsing in a food processor or by covering them with a clean tea towel and bashing them with a rolling pin or similar blunt instrument.

2 To make the spice paste, heat a dry frying pan or saucepan, add the coriander seeds, star anise, cardamom pods and chilli flakes and gently toast for a few minutes, stirring, until they release their aroma. Remove from the pan and grind the spices with a pestle and mortar or electric spice grinder.

3 Blend the ground spices with the remaining spice paste ingredients and 75g (2¾oz) of the toasted macadamias in a food processor or using a stick blender fitted with the chopping/drum attachment.

>>

SERVES 6

150g (5½oz) macadamia nuts
3 pak choi, quartered
50g (1¾oz) green beans
½ mango, stoned, peeled and
   finely sliced
50g (1¾oz) bean sprouts
20g (¾oz) leafy coriander tops

FOR THE SPICE PASTE
1 tablespoon coriander seeds
2 star anise
10 green cardamom pods
¼ teaspoon chilli flakes
3–4 garlic cloves, depending
   on size, peeled
10g (¼oz) fresh root ginger,
   peeled
10g (¼oz) fresh root galangal,
   peeled
1–2 red chillies (20g/¾oz
   total weight)
4 kaffir lime leaves, finely
   deveined and shredded
2 teaspoons dark red gluten-
   free miso paste
2 tablespoons vegetable oil
2 tablespoons sesame oil

FOR THE SAUCE
½ red chilli, thinly sliced
25g (1oz) palm sugar or raw
   coconut sugar (or 20g/¾oz
   soft light brown sugar)
50ml (2fl oz) tamari (gluten-
   free) or dark soy sauce
1½ tablespoons Asian sweet
   tamarind concentrate

1 tablespoon tomato purée

600ml (20fl oz) Dark
  Vegetable Stock (*see page*
  251) or hot water with 1 dark
  vegetable stock cube
  dissolved in it

400ml (14fl oz) can full-fat
  coconut milk

300g (10½oz) peeled and,
  if large, halved new potatoes

1–2 carrots, peeled, halved
  and sliced

2 lemon grass stalks, kept
  whole but with the ends
  bruised

salt

TO SERVE

steamed rice or rice noodles

1 lime, cut into wedges

4   To make the sauce, dry-fry the spice paste in a large saucepan over a gentle heat for 5-8 minutes, stirring, then mix in the chilli, sugar, tamari or soy sauce, tamarind, tomato purée, stock and coconut milk until well combined.

5   At this stage, for a really smooth curry, remove the pan from the heat, pour the mixture into a blender and blend for 3-4 minutes until completely smooth. This is because when making your own spice paste it is very hard to achieve a very fine paste using domestic equipment. However, if you don't mind having a few fibrous bits in there, you can skip this step.

6   Return the mixture to the heat and add the remaining ingredients for the sauce, seasoning to taste with salt. Bring up to a simmer and cook for 30-40 minutes, uncovered, until the potatoes are fully cooked.

7   When you are ready to serve, add the pak choi, green beans and half the mango and cook for about 2-3 minutes until the beans are beginning to soften.

8   Serve with steamed rice or rice noodles, topped with the bean sprouts, remaining mango, coriander and the remaining toasted macadamias, along with lime wedges.

BUTTERNUT SQUASH & TOFU TERRINE
WITH REDCURRANT STUFFING
& ORANGE GLAZE

A very successful Christmas special, this terrine is beautiful and will look fantastic in the centre of any special-occasion table (*see* photograph overleaf). The recipe is a little labour-intensive, but several stages – the glaze, tofu and stuffing – can be prepared in advance. Anyway, the festive season is all about that little bit of extra effort.

The first stage is to hang two blocks of tofu for a minimum of 12 hours, so bear that in mind. Also note that the only tofu that will work for this recipe is Chinese-style fresh tofu (*see* page 81).

Achiote paste is a Mexican paste with a sharp, sour tang (*see* page 248), widely available online, but if you can't get it, don't worry because it's not essential.

Serve the terrine with Truffled Roast Potatoes (*see* page 153), Roast Brussels Sprouts with Smoky Maple Chestnuts (*see* page 150) and White Wine Gravy (*see* page 250).

1   Start by draining the tofu for the butternut tofu. Crush the blocks of tofu with your hands. Follow the instructions for the Soya Labneh on page 246 to hang the tofu in a muslin pouch to drain in the refrigerator for 12 hours or overnight.

2   Meanwhile, roast the butternut squash, used in the stuffing and for the tofu. Preheat the oven to 200°C (400°F), Gas Mark 6. Toss the squash with the oil in a large bowl. Spread out on a baking tray and roast for 10-15 minutes until the squash is fully cooked. Remove from the oven and leave to cool.

3   Blend all the ingredients for the orange glaze in a blender or in a measuring jug with a stick blender. If you don't have either, chop the garlic and herbs very finely by hand and then mix with the other ingredients.

4   Next prepare the redcurrant stuffing mixture. Reserving 200g (7oz) of the roasted butternut squash for the tofu, add the rest to a large bowl with all the stuffing ingredients and mix together, crushing the mixture a little with your hands.

>>

SERVES 6

FOR THE BUTTERNUT TOFU
2 × 325g (11½oz) packs Chinese-style fresh firm tofu
1 butternut squash, peeled, deseeded and cut into small cubes
2 tablespoons olive oil, plus extra for oiling
2 French onion stock cubes, crumbled, or good-quality vegan stock powder
6 sage leaves, finely chopped
1 tablespoon crushed garlic
2 teaspoons garlic powder
pinch of ground white pepper
salt

FOR THE ORANGE GLAZE
250ml (9fl oz) orange juice
75ml (5 tablespoons) maple syrup
¼ teaspoon achiote paste
2 sprigs of thyme, leaves picked
2 sage leaves
2 garlic cloves, peeled
salt and pepper

FOR THE REDCURRANT STUFFING

200g (7oz) caramelized onions

250g (9oz) cooked and peeled chestnuts

1 punnet redcurrants, picked (about 40 redcurrants), but 1 stem reserved for garnish

6 sage leaves, plus extra to garnish

pinch of grated nutmeg

¼ teaspoon ground cinnamon

1 tablespoon chopped flat leaf parsley

2 tablespoons maple syrup

100g (3½oz) fresh white breadcrumbs

TO SERVE

Truffled Roast Potatoes (*see* page 153)

Roast Brussels Sprouts with Smoky Maple Chestnuts (*see* page 150)

White Wine Gravy (*see* page 250)

5   For the butternut tofu, blend the reserved roasted squash with 150ml (5fl oz) of the orange glaze, the stock powder and sage in a blender or in a measuring jug with a stick blender. Then mix with the tofu, crushed garlic, garlic powder, white pepper and salt to taste in a large bowl.

6   Preheat the oven to 190°C (375°F), Gas Mark 5. Brush a 1-litre (1¾-pint) loaf tin (about 10 × 25cm/4 × 10 inches) with olive oil.

7   Press two-thirds of the butternut tofu mixture into the oiled tin and up the sides to a depth of 1.5cm (⅝ inch), leaving a large hollow in the middle. Place the stuffing in the hollow and top with the remaining tofu mixture to seal it in. Bake for 40-45 minutes.

8   Remove the terrine from the oven, turn out of the tin into a shallow baking dish and baste with the some of the remaining orange glaze, then return to the oven. Cook for a further 20 minutes, basting with the rest of the glaze every 5 minutes.

9   Garnish the terrine with the reserved stem of redcurrants and sage leaves before serving with the roast potatoes, Brussels sprouts with chestnuts and gravy.

PIDES

Fantastic for parties, pides are small Turkish flatbreads that have a thin layer of topping similar to a pizza (*see* photograph overleaf). They are sized for individual portions and are traditionally a distinctive almond shape with turned-over edges, though what form they take is really up to you.

We have provided a recipe for the flatbread and several topping suggestions (continued on page 108), including a tomato and vegan cheese one that is great for children (we would make these a little smaller – you should get 12 out of this recipe). If you have a pizza stone for your barbecue, you can cook the pides on that, which is a close approximation to the authentic wood ovens these are traditionally cooked in.

PIDE BASE

1   Mix the yeast with the measured warm water, olive oil and sugar in small bowl or jug and leave somewhere fairly warm to activate for about 15 minutes until beginning to froth.

2   Measure the flours and salt into a large bowl, or into the bowl of a stand mixer fitted with the dough hook, and mix to combine, on a low speed if using a mixer. Then gradually add the yeast mixture and mix to combine.

3   Knead the dough using your mixer on a medium speed for 2 minutes, or on an oiled surface by hand for 5-8 minutes, until smooth and soft.

4   Oil a large bowl and place the dough in the bowl. Cover tightly with clingfilm and leave in a warm place in the kitchen for 3-5 hours.

5   To cook, preheat the oven to 240°C (475°F), Gas Mark 9, or as high as it will go. Heat 2 heavy-based baking trays in the oven. Alternatively, place your pizza stone on the barbecue stoked to a high heat and leave for 20 minutes or so to achieve an even high heat.

6   Divide the dough into the desired number of pides and roll out on a fairly heavily floured surface into your desired shape (*see* recipe introduction). Thinly cover with your sauce and topping of choice, then scoop on to the hot tray or pizza stone using a pizza paddle or a very thin baking sheet with no lip – the removable base of a quiche tin works well.

7   Bake for 5-8 minutes until the base is cooked through and crisp.

>>

PIDE BASE

7g (⅓oz) sachet fast-action dried yeast

300ml (10fl oz) warm water

2 tablespoons olive oil, plus extra for oiling

½ teaspoon sugar

250g (9oz) strong white flour, plus extra (or plain flour) for dusting

225g (8oz) plain flour

1 teaspoon salt

SUN-BLUSHED TOMATO SAUCE

250g (9oz) sun-blushed tomatoes, partially drained of oil

5 basil leaves

1 sprig of oregano, leaves picked

SIMPLE TOMATO SAUCE

olive oil

I small onion, finely diced

1-2 garlic cloves, sliced

1 sprig of oregano, leaves picked and roughly chopped

400g (14oz) can chopped tomatoes

1 tablespoon tomato purée

¼ teaspoon sugar

5 basil leaves, torn into pieces

GRILLED AUBERGINE, SUN-BLUSHED TOMATO AND CAPER

2 aubergines, sliced into 1cm (½-inch) rounds

1 teaspoon sea salt flakes

olive oil

Sun-blushed Tomato Sauce (*see* above)

2 tablespoons lilliput capers or roughly chopped large capers

SAUCES

The first recipe is a simple no-cook sauce that has tons of flavour; the second is a cooked herb-flavoured tomato sauce.

SUN-BLUSHED TOMATO SAUCE

1 Blend all the ingredients in a food processor until you have a chunky paste.

SIMPLE TOMATO SAUCE

1 Warm a glug of olive oil in a medium-sized saucepan, add the onion and garlic and cook over a medium heat for a few minutes, stirring frequently, until the onion is nearly translucent. Add the oregano and cook for a further 2-3 minutes.

2 Add the chopped tomatoes, tomato purée and sugar and bring to a simmer. Cover and cook over a low heat for about 15-20 minutes, stirring frequently. Remove the lid and cook for a further 10 minutes until the sauce has reduced slightly.

3 Remove from the heat, add the basil and blend a little with a stick blender until you have a chunky sauce.

TOPPINGS

You can top the pides with whatever you wish. We find grilled vegetables work well, and here are some other combinations that we really like.

GRILLED AUBERGINE, SUN-BLUSHED TOMATO & CAPER

1 Sprinkle the aubergine rounds with the salt in a bowl or colander and leave to sit for 20-30 minutes until they begin to sweat. Rinse and then squeeze thoroughly to remove the moisture. Toss in a little olive oil.

2 Heat up a griddle pan or your barbecue to a medium heat and grill the aubergines for around 3 minutes on each side until fully cooked and nicely chargrill marked.

3 To assemble, spread your pide dough bases with a thin layer of the sun-blushed tomato sauce and add 2-3 aubergine slices to each. Scatter with the capers and cook according to the instructions opposite.

>>

GRILLED FIELD MUSHROOM, SUN-BLUSHED TOMATOES & PIQUILLO PEPPER

1   Toss the mushrooms in a little olive oil and season with the salt.

2   Heat up a griddle pan or your barbecue to a high heat and grill the mushrooms for around 3 minutes on each side until cooked and nicely chargrill marked.

3   Leave until cool enough to handle, then cut into slices 1cm (½ inch) thick.

4   To assemble, spread your pide dough bases with a thin layer of the sun-blushed tomato sauce and add 4-5 mushroom slices and 3-4 pepper slices to each. Cook according to the instructions on page 104.

ARTICHOKE, CASHEW CREAM & ROCKET

1   Drain the artichokes and cut in half, then cut into slices about 1cm (½ inch) thick.

2   To assemble, spread your pide bases with a thin layer of the cashew cream, reserving a little for serving, and add 3-6 artichoke slices to each, depending on their size. Drizzle over a little olive oil. Cook according to the instructions on page 104.

3   Remove from the heat, then top with the rocket and drizzle over a little more cashew cream before serving.

>>

GRILLED FIELD MUSHROOM, SUN-BLUSHED TOMATOES AND PIQUILLO PEPPER

6 large portobello or flat mushrooms, washed and trimmed

olive oil

pinch of sea salt flakes

Sun-blushed Tomato Sauce (*see* page 105)

8 piquillo peppers from a jar or other jarred roasted and skinned red peppers, drained and thinly sliced

ARTICHOKE, CASHEW CREAM AND ROCKET

8 good-quality Roman artichokes in oil

1 batch of Cashew Cream (*see* page 248)

olive oil

100g (3½oz) rocket

GRILLED BROCCOLI, CHILLI, TAHINI AND DUKKAH

300g (10½oz) Tenderstem
    broccoli (2–3 stems per
    person)
olive oil
1 red chilli, thinly sliced
1 batch of Spiced Tahini Sauce
    (*see* page 80)
Hazelnut and Almond Dukkah
    (*see* page 196), for sprinkling
sea salt flakes

KID-FRIENDLY TOMATO AND VEGAN CHEESE

Simple Tomato Sauce (*see*
    page 105)
200g (7oz) vegan cheese,
    mozzarella-style if available
    or a medium Cheddar type,
    grated

GRILLED BROCCOLI, CHILLI, TAHINI & DUKKAH

1   Toss the broccoli in a little olive oil with the chilli slices, then season with sea salt.

2   Heat up a griddle pan or your barbecue to a high heat and grill the broccoli for around 1–2 minutes on each side until cooked and nicely chargrill marked. If the grilled broccoli stems are very thin, cut them into 5cm (2-inch) batons. If they are thick, slice them in half lengthways first and then into batons.

3   To assemble, spread your pide bases with a thin layer of the tahini sauce and add 4–5 broccoli batons to each, making sure everyone gets a bit of chilli, then sprinkle with a little of the dukkah. Cook according to the instructions on page 104.

KID-FRIENDLY TOMATO & VEGAN CHEESE

1   To assemble, spread your pide bases with a thin layer of the tomato sauce and add some grated vegan cheese to each. Cook according to the instructions on page 104.

KIMCHI BURGER

Tempeh originates from Indonesia and is made from whole fermented soya beans. It can be used in similar ways to tofu and has a satisfying chunky texture. Combining tempeh with kimchi in this burger means that it's full of fantastic fermented antioxidants and natural protein.

We realize kimchi is something of an acquired taste, so if you would prefer a milder-flavoured burger, you can replace it with a 220g (8oz) mix of grated carrots and shredded pak choi.

1   Heat a splash of oil in a frying pan, add the tempeh pieces and cook over a medium heat for 10-12 minutes, turning occasionally, until they begin to colour and become slightly crispy. Add the baby corn, garlic, ginger, chilli and salt and cook for a further 3-4 minutes, stirring frequently. Leave to cool.

2   Meanwhile, preheat the oven to 180°C (350°F), Gas Mark 4.

3   Mix together the breadcrumbs, gram flour, spring onions, coriander, kimchi and cracked pepper in a large bowl. Add the cooked tempeh mixture, crumbling the tempeh pieces between your fingers so that it resembles a fine mince, and mix together well, compressing the mixture with your hands until it holds together.

4   Shape the mixture into 4-6 patties.

5   Heat a good glug of oil in a large frying pan, add the burgers and fry over a medium heat for 3-4 minutes on each side until dark brown. Transfer to a baking tray and finish cooking in the oven for 12-15 minutes.

6   While waiting for the burgers to cook, get your accompaniments ready and toast your buns.

7   Assemble your burgers and serve straight away.

MAKES 4-6 BURGERS

light oil (such as groundnut or sunflower), for frying

200g (7oz) tempeh, diced into 2cm (¾-inch) cubes

100g (3½oz) baby corn, thinly sliced into discs

1 large garlic clove (10g/¼oz)

15g (½oz) fresh root ginger, peeled and grated or finely chopped

1 red chilli, finely diced

½ teaspoon salt

120g (4¼oz) stale white breadcrumbs

15g (½oz) gram flour

4 spring onions, sliced

20g (¾oz) coriander, chopped

250g (9oz) Kimchi (*see page 126*)

¼ teaspoon cracked black pepper

TO SERVE

200g (7oz) Kimchi (*see page 126*)

mayonnaise or Roast Garlic Aioli (*see page 181*)

¼ iceberg lettuce, leaves separated

4-6 burger buns

MEMPHIS BOURBON BARBECUE SKEWERS

This dish makes a satisfying main course when paired with our Ranch Dip (*see* page 174) and sides of Rainbow Root Slaw (*see* page 140), Charred Leeks and Peppers (*see* page 56) and Levant-spiced Barbecue Cauliflower (*see* page 144). Alternatively, the skewers just on their own with some of the slaw and dip proved an instant success as a starter on our menu. The heat from the dry rub is well balanced by the sweet sticky barbecue glaze and the refreshing root veg slaw.

1 For the dry rub, combine all the spices in a bowl, then grind in an electric spice grinder to form a fine powder. Set aside.

2 Slice each block of tofu into 6–7 pieces across its width. Dip each piece lightly in the dry rub and then leave to rest on a wire rack for 30–40 minutes to allow the dry rub to set.

3 While the tofu is resting, make the Bourbon Barbecue Sauce (*see* page 195).

4 Meanwhile, preheat the oven to 190°C (375°F), Gas Mark 5.

5 Once the tofu has rested for the required time, bake on the wire rack (so that the air can circulate around the tofu) for 40–50 minutes until the tofu has firmed up slightly, turning the tofu once midway through cooking. Remove from the oven and leave to cool.

6 Preheat the oven grill to a medium heat. Using 6 or 7 bamboo kebab sticks, thread 2 slices of the baked tofu on to each stick and place on a baking sheet. Brush the tofu on one side generously with the barbecue sauce, place on the middle shelf of the oven and grill for 4–5 minutes until the sauce begins to bubble and caramelize slightly. Remove from the heat, turn the skewers over and brush with more of the sauce, then grill for 4–5 minutes. You can glaze and then grill each side again for a more intense barbecue flavour.

7 Serve with ranch dip and a selection of side dishes.

SERVES 4

2 × 325g (11½oz) packs Chinese-style fresh firm tofu
1 quantity Bourbon Barbecue Sauce (*see* page 195)

FOR THE DRY RUB
1 teaspoon chilli flakes
1 tablespoon sweet paprika
1 tablespoon smoked paprika
1 tablespoon garlic powder
1 tablespoon sea salt flakes
1 tablespoon cumin seeds
1 tablespoon ground cinnamon
½ tablespoon black peppercorns
1 tablespoon soft light brown sugar
1 tablespoon Mexican or regular dried oregano

TO SERVE
Ranch Dip (*see* page 174)
Rainbow Root Slaw (*see* page 140)
Charred Leeks and Peppers (*see* page 56)
Levant-spiced Barbecue Cauliflower (*see* page 144)

BOWLS

TOKYO BOWL

A Japanese-inspired feast of fantastic colours and sweet tangy and spicy flavours, the Tokyo Bowl includes spicy tofu, plum teriyaki baby aubergines, pickled daikon (mooli), black rice, a mix of toasted seeds and seaweed and edamame. The dish is finished with a warming cup of miso soup, which can either be drunk with it or poured over the bowl.

BLACK RICE

We love black Venus rice, a variant of glutinous rice also referred to as black Thai rice or black jasmine rice. The colour is just amazing and it has a lovely nutty flavour. It's available in some supermarkets and from online suppliers, but if you can't find it, you can substitute sushi or brown rice or soba noodles.

1   Rinse the rice and then drain.
2   Bring the measured water to the boil in a saucepan. Add the rice and return to a simmer.
3   Cover the pan and simmer for about 30-45 minutes until all the water has been absorbed and the rice is cooked.

TERIAYKI-MARINATED TOFU

This recipe will make a bit more teriyaki sauce than you need for the aubergines, so save the rest for delicious stir-fries. The plums don't have to be super ripe - if they are harder, your teriyaki will just be a little more tart. You can add more sugar if you prefer a sweeter sauce.

1   Mix the mirin and tamari together in a bowl. Add the tofu and toss to coat well. Cover with clingfilm and leave to marinate in the refrigerator for at least an hour.
2   Preheat the oven to 180°C (350°F), Gas Mark 4. Line a baking tray with baking parchment.
3   Remove the tofu from the marinade, reserving the marinade for the Plum Teriyaki Aubergine (see opposite). Spread the tofu out on the lined baking tray. Mix the spice mix, sesame seeds, sesame oil and agave together in a bowl and drizzle the mixture over the tofu. Bake for 20-25 minutes until the tofu firms up slightly and the alcohol has been cooked out.

SERVES 4-6

BLACK RICE
200g (7oz) black Venus rice
450ml (16fl oz) water
salt

TERIYAKI-MARINATED TOFU
200ml (7fl oz) mirin
50ml (2fl oz) tamari
325g (11½oz) pack firm tofu,
    cut into cubes
2 teaspoons Japanese seven
    spice mix (*shichimi togarashi*)
2 teaspoons black sesame seeds
1 tablespoon sesame oil
1 tablespoon agave syrup

>>

PLUM TERIYAKI AUBERGINE

teriyaki marinade reserved
   from the Teriyaki-marinated
   Tofu (*see* opposite)
3 plums (150g/5½oz total
   weight), stoned and diced
1 tablespoon coconut or caster
   sugar, or to taste
10–12 baby aubergines or
   2 regular aubergines
75ml (5 tablespoons) blended
   oil (half sesame and half
   sunflower)
salt

SIMPLE PICKLED DAIKON

1 large or 2 small daikon
   (mooli) (800g/1lb 12oz total
   weight), peeled and sliced
½ tablespoon sea salt flakes
250ml (9fl oz) rice vinegar
100ml (3½fl oz) water
150ml (5fl oz) mirin
1 tablespoon sugar
1 tablespoon sea salt flakes
30g (1oz) peeled fresh root
   ginger, sliced
½ tablespoon turmeric
½ tablespoon dried wakame
   seaweed

PLUM TERIYAKI AUBERGINE

1   Add the reserved marinade to a small saucepan along with the plums and sugar and simmer for 8–10 minutes until the plums have softened and are fully cooked. Remove from the heat and blend in a food processor or with a stick blender. Taste for sweetness and add more sugar if needed, as plums can be on the sour side.

2   Cut the aubergines in half and score the cut sides in a cross-cross pattern, cutting almost all the way down through the flesh but without piercing the skin. Place in a bowl or colander, sprinkle lightly with salt and leave to sit for an hour. Rinse the aubergines and place in a bowl with the oil, then toss to coat the aubergines well.

3   Preheat the oven to 200°C (400°F), Gas Mark 6. Heat a large frying pan to a medium-high heat, add the oiled aubergines and fry for about 2–3 minutes on each side to give them some colour. Transfer to a baking tray and coat with the marinade, spreading it over the aubergines with your fingers to allow the marinade to soak into the flesh. Bake for 20–30 minutes until the aubergine flesh is soft and the sauce has caramelized slightly.

SIMPLE PICKLED DAIKON

Daikon, also known as mooli, is a long white radish about the length of a cucumber. If you can't find it, you can achieve a similar effect with peeled and sliced turnips. Pickles are a key part of Japanese cuisine, giving a refreshing palate-cleansing effect.

1   Place the daikon slices in a bowl and sprinkle with the salt. Leave to stand for 30 minutes.

2   Rinse with cold water and squeeze out all the excess liquid, then place in an airtight sturdy plastic food container or a sterilized glass jar (*see* page 126).

3   Combine all the remaining ingredients in a small stainless steel saucepan and bring to the boil, then reduce the heat and simmer for 5 minutes.

4   Pour the hot pickling liquid over the daikon, leave to cool and then seal. Store in the refrigerator for up to a week.

>>

MISO SOUP

100ml (3½fl oz) water

1 tablespoon dark red miso
    paste per person

1 teaspoon dried wakame
    seaweed per person

SEED-WEED

50g (1¾oz) sesame seeds

50g (1¾oz) pumpkin seeds

50g (1¾oz) sunflower seeds

25g (1oz) hemp seeds

25g (1oz) chia seeds

2 tablespoons agave syrup

4 teaspoons tamari

4 teaspoons sesame oil

30g (1oz) (2 sheets) nori
    seaweed, chopped and
    blended in a food processor
    or chopped by hand into
    small pieces

TO SERVE

200g (7oz) cooked shelled
    edamame beans, cooled

8 spring onions, finely sliced

MISO SOUP

1   Bring the measured water to the boil in a small saucepan,
    stir in the miso and wakame and simmer for 5 minutes.

SEED-WEED

We just love this! It's delicious on stir-fries and salads, not to
mention being jam-packed with goodness. You can chop and
change the seeds in this recipe according to your preference,
but just keep the total quantity to around 200g (7oz).

1   Preheat the oven to 170°C (340°F), Gas Mark 3½.

2   Mix all the ingredients, except the nori, together in a bowl and
    then spread out on a baking sheet.

3   Bake for 15 minutes, stirring occasionally.

4   Add the nori, tossing to mix, and bake for a further 5 minutes.

5   Remove from the oven and leave to cool, then store in a clean
    airtight jar or other container in a cool, dry place. It will keep
    for up to 3 weeks.

TO ASSEMBLE

1   Each bowl should get a scoop of rice, some aubergine, a few
    cubes of tofu, a cup of miso soup and a couple of tablespoons
    of seed-weed, finishing with a scoop of edamame and spring
    onions, along with a heaped tablespoon of cold pickled daikon
    (about 4-5 slices) on the side of the bowl.

PUEBLA BOWL

This makes a great summer lunch or evening meal. The food of Mexico, so rich in herbs, fruits and vegetables yet filling with hearty beans, is perfect for a conversion to a vegan diet. The Puebla Bowl is comprised of spiced black beans, avocado lime cream, grilled pineapple and soft corn taco, raw corn salsa and quinoa with our own Chihuahua cheese made with almonds. Real Chihuahua cheese is pretty much impossible to buy in Britain (believe us, we've tried!), but it's very close in flavour to feta, so we adapted our vegan almond feta recipe to fit (see pages 242–3). But if you don't have time to make it, don't worry, as you'll find plenty of flavours going on without it.

SPICED BLACK BEANS

These are our version of refried beans, but as these aren't actually refried, they are much healthier. Epazote is a dried Mexican herb used in bean dishes to give them fewer undesirable after effects (less said about that the better) and lends a very authentic edge to our Mexican dishes. It is available online but if you can't find it, just omit it from the recipe. Equally, Mexican oregano has a slightly milder finish than regular dried oregano, so if you can't find it, use a bit less of regular dried or fresh oregano.

1   If using dried beans, drain and rinse the soaked beans, then place in a large saucepan, cover with plenty of fresh water and add a little salt. Bring to the boil and boil for 10 minutes, skimming off any foam. Reduce the heat and simmer for up to an hour until the beans have softened but are slightly firm to the bite, then drain.

2   Heat a medium-sized saucepan with the oil, add the onion with the cumin seeds and sauté over a gentle heat for a few minutes, stirring.

3   Add the beans, measured water, oregano and epazote and bring to a simmer. Add the bicarbonate of soda, salt and stock cube, cover and cook the beans for 1 hour–1 hour 10 minutes, stirring frequently, until they are beginning to break down.

>>

SERVES 4–6

SPICED BLACK BEANS
400g (14oz) can black beans, drained and rinsed, or 90g (3¼oz) dried black turtle beans, soaked in cold water preferably overnight but for at least 5 hours, then cooked (see method)
1 tablespoon vegetable oil
½ small onion, finely diced
½ teaspoon crushed cumin seeds
200ml (7fl oz) water
¼ teaspoon Mexican oregano
⅛ teaspoon epazote
¼ teaspoon bicarbonate of soda
¼ teaspoon salt
¼ French onion stock cube, crumbled

QUINOA SALAD

400ml (14fl oz) water

200g (7oz) quinoa

½ teaspoon salt

1 tablespoon olive oil

grated zest of 1 lime

200g (7oz) Almond Chihuahua
  (see page 243), crumbled

40g (1½oz) coriander, chopped

½ small red chilli, finely
  chopped

AVOCADO LIME CREAM

2 avocados, stoned and peeled

juice of 1 lime

about 200ml (7fl oz) light
  coconut milk (or use the
  thinner liquid from canned
  full-fat coconut milk that
  separates from the cream –
  see page 237)

salt

RAW CORN SALSA

2 corn on the cobs, husks and
  fibres removed

1 red chilli, finely diced

1 small or ½ medium red onion,
  finely diced

40g (1½oz) coriander, chopped

grated zest and juice of 1 lime

salt

QUINOA SALAD

The ancient grain of the Andes, quinoa is packed with nutrients and has a pleasant crunchy finish when cooked in the right way. Available in white, black and red, choose whichever colour you prefer; we use a rainbow mixture.

1   Bring the measured water to the boil in a small saucepan and add the quinoa and salt, then cover, reduce the heat and simmer for 15 minutes until the water has been absorbed. The quinoa should still have some bite to it.

2   Remove from the heat, then toss with the olive oil. Return to the pan off the heat, cover and leave to sit and steam for 10–15 minutes.

3   Uncover, fluff up with a fork and leave to cool.

4   Put the quinoa in a bowl, add the remaining ingredients and toss to combine.

AVOCADO LIME CREAM

1   Blend the ingredients in a food processor, adding the coconut milk in stages, until you achieve a thick double cream consistency – you should be able to pour it over the finished bowl. Season to taste with salt.

2   Alternatively, use a potato masher to mash the avocados in a large bowl as smoothly as possible, then use a balloon whisk to beat in the lime juice and coconut milk in stages, seasoning to taste with salt.

RAW CORN SALSA

If you've never eaten raw corn before, we think you'll be pleasantly surprised by this salsa. It's so sweet and crunchy, you'll almost wonder why you ever bothered cooking it.

1   Wash the corn cobs, then cut off the kernels by holding the cob upright with its base on the chopping board and slicing from the top downwards with a sharp knife. Don't cut too close to the cob, as this part can be a bit fibrous. Combine with the other ingredients.

>>

I baby or ½ small pineapple,
   skin and core removed, then
   cut into semicircular slices
   about 1cm (½ inch) thick
soft corn tacos – allow at least
   1 per person

TO GARNISH
fresh coriander
lime wedges

GRILLED PINEAPPLE & SOFT TACO

If you can't get soft corn tacos, serve this with a handful of tortilla chips instead.

1   Heat a griddle pan over a high heat until smoking and then reduce the heat to achieve an even high heat under the pan.

2   Add the pineapple slices to the hot pan and grill for about 3 minutes until chargrill marks appear on the underside, then turn over and repeat on the other side. Don't move the slices too much. Remove from the pan.

3   Grill the tacos in the pan for just a minute or so on each side.

TO ASSEMBLE

1   Each bowl should have a large scoop of beans, quinoa salad, a few slices of grilled pineapple, the raw corn salsa and a taco. Then drizzle over the avocado cream and garnish with coriander and lime wedges.

KIMCHI BOWL

This filling and warming bowl, perfect for a cold spring day, includes marinated tofu, brown rice, stir-fried pak choi, broccoli and spring onions, peanut sauce, roasted peanuts and, of course, kimchi. Fermented spicy cabbage, kimchi is a staple side dish in Korean cuisine and contains a high concentration of vitamin C, carotene and lactic acid bacteria. And the longer it's fermented, the better it tastes.

KIMCHI

You will need an 850ml-1-litre (1½-1¾-pint) preserving jar for the kimchi, which should be sterilized. Our preferred method is to wash the jar on a quick cycle in the dishwasher and pack the kimchi into the jar while it is still warm.

1 Pour the measured hot water into a large bowl, add the salt and stir to dissolve. Add the Chinese cabbage, pak choi and carrot and massage the vegetables for a few minutes until they begin to absorb the water. Cover with clingfilm and leave to stand at room temperature, preferably overnight or for at least 5-6 hours.

2 Drain and then taste the vegetables - they should be salty but not unpleasantly so. If they are too salty, rinse or soak them in clean water, taste again and repeat until you are happy with the taste.

3 Place the apple, onion, garlic and ginger in a food processor and process to a smooth paste, adding a splash of water so they blend properly. Add the Korean chilli powder and whizz to combine well.

4 Add the spring onions to the brined vegetables along with the paste, and mix together well making sure all the vegetables are coated with the paste.

5 Pack the kimchi tightly into the sterilized glass jar (see recipe introduction), squeezing out most of the air bubbles as you pack the mixture in. Leave a 2.5cm (1-inch) space between the surface of the kimchi and the top of the jar, as the kimchi will expand as it ferments, then seal the jar and keep in a dry, cool place away from any direct sunlight. Leave it for a minimum of 48 hours to allow it to ferment or up to 3 days, tasting it while it's fermenting until it reaches the desired flavour, then transfer to the refrigerator where the fermentation will slow down. Kimchi should tingle slightly on the tongue and taste a little sour.

6 The kimchi should keep in the refrigerator for up to 1 month, but don't use if it forms a mould or turns slimy.

SERVES 4-6

KIMCHI
700ml (1¼ pints) hot water
30g (1oz) salt
½ Chinese cabbage (350g/ 12oz), the leafy part cut into 5cm (2-inch) chunks, the thick base into 2cm (¾-inch) chunks
2 pak choi (350g/12oz total weight), cut into 5cm (2-inch) chunks
1 carrot, peeled and grated
1 dessert apple, cored and roughly chopped
¼ onion, roughly chopped
10g (¼oz) garlic, roughly chopped
10g (¼oz) fresh root ginger, peeled and roughly chopped
1½ tablespoons Korean chilli powder
3 spring onions, sliced

PEANUT SAUCE
120g (4¼oz) crunchy peanut butter
2 tablespoons Asian sweet tamarind concentrate
1 tablespoon coconut sugar
1 small red chilli
30g (1oz) roasted, salted peanuts, crushed, plus extra if desired
200ml (7fl oz) light or full-fat coconut milk
4 tablespoons tamari
salt (if needed)

>>

PEANUT SAUCE

1 Put all the ingredients in a food processor or blender and blend together until well combined, then check and add salt if needed. Add extra crushed peanuts for a coarser-textured sauce.

TAMARIND-MARINATED TOFU

1 For the marinade, combine the tamari, measured water, tamarind and sugar in a shallow dish.

2 Add the tofu and toss to coat in the marinade, then cover the dish with clingfilm and leave to marinate in the refrigerator for at least an hour.

3 Preheat the oven to 180°C (350°F), Gas Mark 4. Line a baking tray with baking parchment.

4 Remove the tofu from the marinade, reserving the marinade for the Stir-fried Vegetables (*see* below) and other uses, and spread the tofu out on the lined baking tray. Drizzle some of the peanut sauce over the tofu and bake for 20-25 minutes until the tofu firms up slightly.

BROWN RICE

1 Rinse the rice in cold water and drain.

2 Bring the measured water, with the salt added, to the boil in a saucepan. Add the rice and return to a simmer. Cover and simmer over a low heat for about 30-45 minutes until all the water has been absorbed and the rice is cooked. Add more hot water from the kettle if the pan runs dry before the rice has fully cooked.

STIR-FRIED VEGETABLES

1 Heat the sesame oil in a wok over a medium-high heat, add the ginger, garlic and chilli and stir-fry for 20 seconds. Add the vegetables and stir-fry, tossing frequently, for 4-5 minutes until they become tender, adding a little of the reserved tamarind marinade during cooking.

TO ASSEMBLE

1 Each bowl should have a cup of brown rice, a few cubes of tofu, some peanut sauce, stir-fried vegetables and a large spoonful of kimchi, all topped with roasted peanuts, coriander and a lime wedge, if liked.

TAMARIND-MARINATED TOFU
50ml (2fl oz) tamari
50ml (2fl oz) water
1 tablespoon Asian sweet tamarind concentrate
1 tablespoon coconut sugar
325g (11½oz) pack firm tofu, cut into slabs or cubes
Peanut Sauce (*see* above), for drizzling

BROWN RICE
300g (10½oz) wholegrain brown rice
450ml (16fl oz) water
salt

STIR-FRIED VEGETABLES
3 tablespoons sesame oil
50g (1¾oz) peeled fresh root ginger, grated
5 garlic cloves, grated
1 red chilli, finely sliced
4 pak choi, quartered
6 Tenderstem broccoli stems, cut into 5cm (2-inch) batons
8 spring onions, cut into 5cm (2-inch) batons
tamarind marinade reserved from the Tamarind-marinated Tofu (*see* above)

TO SERVE
200g (7oz) whole roasted, salted peanuts
about 100g (3½oz) coriander, leaves picked and roughly chopped
lime wedges (optional)

GOA BOWL

DAHL

150g (5½oz) dried urid beans

100g (3½oz) dried chana dahl
(dried yellow split peas)

150g (5½oz) dried red kidney
beans

75ml (5 tablespoons) light oil
(groundnut or sunflower)

1 onion, diced

3cm (1¼-inch) piece of fresh
root ginger, peeled and
grated, then finely chopped

1 green chilli, diced

½ tablespoon cumin seeds

½ tablespoon toasted and
ground cumin seeds

½ cinnamon stick

½ teaspoon chilli powder

⅓ teaspoon chilli flakes

½ teaspoon toasted and
ground cardamom seeds

¼ teaspoon toasted and
ground whole cloves

good pinch of grated nutmeg

400g (14oz) can chopped
tomatoes, half blended to
a purée

2 bay leaves

1 teaspoon dried fenugreek
leaves (methi)

juice of 1 lime

20g (1¾oz) coriander,
chopped, to garnish

salt

A bowl full of fresh and filling South Indian-inspired goodies – dahl, cardamom and pea basmati, mango chutney, okra, coconut chutney, lime and coriander naan. The dahl in this recipe features a three-bean/pulse mixture that needs a long soak, but it gives a dense, creamy result. For a gluten-free option, omit the Coriander Naan.

DAHL

Madhur Jaffrey says the key to great dahl is the very frequent stirring and we're not going to argue with Madhur. The urid beans, also known as mungo beans or black lentils (not to be confused with the smaller true black lentil), are common to South Indian cuisine and are easy to find in shops with a decent Asian selection and in some supermarkets, or online. For a quicker-cooking version, you can just use 300g (10½oz) dried chana dahl (dried yellow split peas), thoroughly rinsed.

1   Wash the urid beans and dahl, then leave to soak in cold water overnight. Wash and soak the red kidney beans separately.

2   Drain the urid beans and dahl and set aside. Drain the kidney beans, wash again and place in a saucepan. Cover with plenty of fresh water, add a little salt and bring to the boil. Boil rapidly for a good 10 minutes, skimming off any foam, then drain and set aside.

3   Heat the oil in a medium-sized saucepan, add the onion with the ginger and chilli and cook over a medium heat, stirring frequently, until it begins to brown. Add the spices and cook gently, stirring, for a few minutes.

4   Stir in the red kidney beans, urid beans and dahl, then pour in enough water to cover by 2cm (¾ inch). Add the remaining ingredients (except the coriander) and simmer over a medium heat for 45 minutes–1 hour, stirring frequently, until the beans and pulses begin to break down. Add water as necessary, but the dahl should be quite thick and with a creamy consistency. Season to taste with salt.

>>

CARDAMOM AND PEA
   BASMATI RICE

250g (9oz) basmati rice

1 tablespoon light oil (such as
   groundnut or sunflower)

3 green cardamom pods,
   crushed

½ teaspoon nigella seeds

1 teaspoon turmeric

300ml (10fl oz) boiling water

½ teaspoon salt

100g (3½oz) peas or petit pois
   (defrosted if frozen)

CORIANDER NAAN

150ml (5fl oz) soya milk

1 tablespoon melted coconut oil

4 sprigs of coriander, chopped

1 garlic clove, very finely
   chopped or grated

250g (9oz) plain flour, plus
   extra for dusting

2 teaspoons caster sugar

1 teaspoon baking powder

1 teaspoon salt

finely grated zest of 1 lime

1 green chilli, finely chopped

OKRA

2 tablespoons light oil (such as
   groundnut or sunflower)

4–6 okra per person, only hard
   stems trimmed

salt

CARDAMOM & PEA BASMATI RICE

1   Wash the basmati rice well under cold running water for
    5–8 minutes until the water runs clear, then drain.

2   Heat the oil in a small saucepan, add the cardamom, nigella
    seeds and turmeric and lightly fry, stirring, until they release
    their aroma. Stir in the rice, then add the measured boiling
    water and salt. Reduce the heat to low, cover and simmer for
    8–10 minutes until rice is fully cooked.

3   Remove from the heat and stir in the peas.

CORIANDER NAAN

Naan bread is usually made with milk and ghee (clarified
butter), so it's nice to have an easy vegan version, and this is
about as simple as bread gets, with no yeast. And it just cooks
under the grill in a few minutes. This recipe makes 6 naan.

1   Mix the milk, melted coconut oil, coriander and garlic together
    in a jug.

2   Measure out the remaining ingredients into a bowl and stir to
    combine. Make a well in the centre and add the milk mixture,
    then mix together to make a dough.

3   Turn the dough out on to a floured work surface and use the
    palms of your hands to knead for 8–10 minutes.

4   Return the dough to the bowl, cover with clingfilm and leave
    in a warm place to rise for 20–25 minutes.

5   Once the dough has risen and almost doubled in volume, divide into
    6 balls. With a rolling pin, roll out each ball into a teardrop shape.

6   Heat your grill to high. Place the naans under the hot grill, in
    batches, and cook for 2–3 minutes on one side until the surface
    bubbles and begins to colour, then turn over and repeat on the
    other side.

OKRA

Okra cooked fresh is delicious with a lovely crunch, which may
come as a surprise to those people who think of okra as mushy
or slimy. It doesn't have to be. The trick is not to trim the whole
top off but just the hard stem, and not to wash the okra until
just before you cook it.

1   Heat the oil in a wok until very hot. Throw in the okra and cook,
    tossing frequently, for about 2–3 minutes until the colour has
    deepened and they are just beginning to puff up or collapse.

2   Season with salt.

>>

MANGO CHUTNEY

This is a simple fresh chutney with a fantastic bright yellow colour.

1 Heat the oil in a small saucepan, add the onion and sauté over a medium heat, stirring frequently, until browned. Add the ginger and cook for a further few minutes. Stir in the chilli and all the spices except the turmeric and cook gently, stirring, until the spices are lightly toasted.

2 Add all the remaining ingredients and bring to a simmer, then reduce the heat and cook for 30-40 minutes, stirring frequently, especially towards the end of the cooking time to ensure the chutney doesn't stick to the base of the pan. Leave to cool.

3 Store in a sterilized jar (see page 126) or in an airtight sturdy plastic food container in the refrigerator - it will keep for 7-10 days if stored correctly.

COCONUT CHUTNEY

1 Blitz all the ingredients together in a food processor until smooth.

2 Alternatively, chop all the solid ingredients very finely by hand, and crush the toasted coriander seeds, then mix everything together.

TO ASSEMBLE

1 Each serving should comprise a large serving of dahl, a large scoop of basmati rice, a naan bread, a few okra, a small portion of mango chutney and a portion of coconut chutney. Garnish with spring onions, coriander and a lime wedge.

MANGO CHUTNEY

50ml (2fl oz) light oil (such as groundnut or sunflower)

½ small onion, finely diced

5g (⅛oz) peeled fresh root ginger, finely sliced and then cut into batons

¼ red chilli, finely chopped

seeds from 2 green cardamom pods, crushed

½ cinnamon stick

¼ teaspoon cumin seeds

⅛ teaspoon crushed (not ground) coriander seeds

good pinch of nigella seeds

⅛ teaspoon turmeric

1 Bramley apple, peeled, cored and diced

1 mango, stoned, peeled and finely diced

100g (3½oz) caster sugar

⅛ teaspoon salt

100ml (3½fl oz) water

50ml (2fl oz) cider vinegar

COCONUT CHUTNEY

100g (3½oz) desiccated coconut

50g (1¾oz) coriander, chopped

1 small garlic clove, crushed

1 green chilli, finely chopped

10g (¼oz) fresh root ginger, peeled and crushed or finely grated

½ teaspoon coriander seeds, toasted in a dry pan

½ teaspoon salt

200ml (7fl oz) soya yogurt

200ml (7fl oz) light coconut milk

juice of 1 lime

TO GARNISH

2 spring onions, sliced

fresh coriander

lime wedges

SOUL BOWL

SERVES 4-6

QUINOA SALAD

2 tablespoons agave syrup

2 tablespoons cider vinegar

1 tablespoon light olive oil

1 litre (1¾ pints) water

150g (5½oz) quinoa

pinch of salt

200g (7oz) cherry tomatoes, halved

100g (3½oz) peeled carrot, grated

100g (3½oz) peeled beetroot, grated

50g (1¾oz) pitted dried dates, chopped

50g (1¾oz) flat leaf parsley, chopped

40g (1½oz) mint, chopped

SHIITAKI AND KALE SALAD WITH TAMARI DRESSING

2 tablespoons tamari

2 tablespoons water

1 teaspoon sesame oil

1 teaspoon rice vinegar

150g (5½oz) shiitake mushrooms, sliced

splash of light olive oil

150g (5½oz) baby kale or regular kale stripped of its stems

Talented chef Nadia Lim (nadialim.com), from New Zealand, provided us with the inspiration for this winning ensemble. It's her recipe we have adapted here to create a fresh salad bowl packed to the hilt with nutritious ingredients.

Comprised of two salads - a shiitaki and kale salad and a quinoa salad with carrot, beetroot and tomato - it also comes with our Cashew Cream (see page 248), avocado, sprouts, toasted seeds and sliced radishes. Although we like to present it altogether as a bowl, you could serve the various components separately to make a lovely summer spread.

QUINOA SALAD

1 Mix together the agave syrup, cider vinegar, 1 tablespoon water and olive oil to make a dressing and set aside.

2 Bring the measured water to the boil in a saucepan and add the quinoa and salt, then cover, reduce the heat and simmer for 10-15 minutes. The quinoa should still have some bite to it.

3 Drain the quinoa in a sieve and leave to air-dry for 10-15 minutes until it has dried out, then fluff up slightly with a fork and leave to finish cooling.

4 Once cool, add to a bowl with the remaining salad ingredients and the dressing and mix together well.

SHIITAKI & KALE SALAD WITH TAMARI DRESSING

1 Mix together the tamari, measured water, sesame oil and rice vinegar to make a dressing and set aside.

2 Preheat the oven to 200°C (400°F), Gas Mark 6.

3 Toss the shiitake mushrooms in the oil, spread out on a baking tray and cook for 8-10 minutes until fully cooked. Remove from the oven and leave to cool.

4 Add the shiitake to a bowl with the baby kale and the dressing and mix together well. If using regular kale, you will first need to chiffonade the leaves - stack them, roll them and then finely slice them. These leaves are not as tender as the baby kale, so will need to be firmly massaged with the dressing and set aside for 15-20 minutes, then massaged with the dressing again before serving.

>>

TO SERVE

50g (1¾oz) mixed toasted
   sunflower and pumpkin seeds

1½ tablespoons mixed toasted
   black and white sesame seeds

½ ripe Hass avocado per
   person

150–200g (5½–7oz) Cashew
   Cream (*see* page 248)

30g (1oz) sprouts (we use
   China Rose radish sprouts)

200g (7oz) radishes, thinly
   sliced

TO ASSEMBLE

1   Place an equal portion of each salad in a bowl, sprinkling the
    quinoa salad with the toasted sunflower and pumpkin seeds and
    the shiitake and kale salad with the toasted black and white
    sesame seeds.

2   Peel and slice each avocado half, then add to the salad along
    with the cashew cream, sprouts and radishes.

SIDES

WASABI SLAW

This recipe comes from one of our head chefs, Agnes Wala, who has previously been in charge of our insanely busy salad bar at our Soho branch. The lovely crunchy texture of the wasabi peas and the kick of the wasabi mayo make for an interesting twist on a traditional slaw. It's great served as a barbecue side or with Drunken Tempura-battered Silken Tofu (*see* page 88) or the Kimchi Burger (*see* page 110).

As an alternative to Chinese cabbage, you could use a mild-flavoured green cabbage such as Savoy or white.

1   Shred the fennel and cabbages very finely.

2   Grate the carrots on the large-holed side of a box grater.

3   Toss the fennel, cabbage, carrots and bean sprouts together in a large bowl and add the sesame oil and enough of the mayo to coat but not smother.

4   Crush the vegetables with your hands a little so that they break down slightly.

5   Crush the wasabi peas coarsely using a pestle and mortar or by placing in a bowl and crushing with the end of a rolling pin or similar blunt instrument.

6   Add most of the wasabi peas, spring onions and coriander to the bowl, reserving some for garnishing. Mix through the slaw.

7   Top the slaw with the remaining crushed wasabi peas, spring onions and coriander.

SERVES 4–6

½ fennel bulb, trimmed
    and cored
200g (7oz) Chinese cabbage,
    cored
½ Hispi (pointed) cabbage,
    cored
2 carrots, peeled
50g (1¾oz) bean sprouts
2 tablespoons sesame oil
100–150ml (3½–5fl oz) Wasabi
    Mayo (*see* page 181)
80g (3oz) wasabi peas
6 spring onions, finely chopped
1 small bunch of coriander,
    roughly chopped

RAINBOW ROOT SLAW
WITH ORANGE, MAPLE & THYME DRESSING

This is a fantastic colourful side dish in which the glossy dressing makes the colours really shine, and is ideal for serving with the Buffalo-marinated Tofu with Crunchy Crumb Coating (*see* page 48) or Memphis Bourbon Barbecue Skewers (*see* page 112).

The vegetables can be changed for any you prefer – try kohlrabi or celeriac – and the apple could be swapped for a pear.

1 Very finely shred the cabbage and fennel, then put in a large bowl.
2 Grate the apple, parsnips, beetroot and carrots on the large-holed side of a box grater. Add to the bowl and mix together.
3 Add enough dressing to the vegetables and apple to coat them but not make them soggy. Crush the vegetables with your hands a little so that they break down slightly.
4 Finally, add the currants and mix through the slaw.

SERVES 4–6

400g (14oz) red cabbage, tough outer leaves removed
½ fennel bulb, trimmed and cored
1 red-skinned dessert apple (such as Red Pippin)
2 parsnips, peeled
1 beetroot, peeled
2 carrots, peeled
½ batch of Orange, Maple and Thyme Dressing (*see* page 186)
40g (1½oz) currants

ROAST TENDERSTEM BROCCOLI
WITH MOJO DE AJO

The marriage of roast broccoli with this delicious garlic sauce is simply magic. This recipe is also a great one for a summer barbecue, where you can cook the broccoli on a hot grill instead of roasting it in the oven. Try serving it with the "Chicken" and Waffles (*see* page 86) or Memphis Bourbon Barbecue Skewers (*see* page 112).

1   Preheat the oven to 220°C (425°F), Gas Mark 7. Put a baking tray in the oven to heat up.

2   Wash and drain the broccoli. then toss with the olive oil, salt and chilli.

3   Spread out in a single layer on the hot baking tray and roast for 4–5 minutes, depending on the thickness of the stems, on each side until the broccoli has coloured and is tender but still al dente.

4   Remove from oven and toss the broccoli with the mojo de ajo, then serve with a few lemon wedges.

SERVES 4–6

450g (1lb) Tenderstem broccoli
1 tablespoon extra virgin olive oil
large pinch of sea salt flakes
¼ red chilli, thinly sliced
4 tablespoons Mojo de Ajo
  (*see* page 185)
lemon wedges, to serve

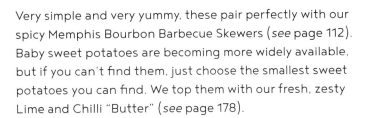

BAKED BABY SWEET POTATOES

SERVES 4-6

1kg (2lb 4oz) or 6 baby
sweet potatoes

2 tablespoons olive oil

1 teaspoon sea salt flakes

4–6 teaspoons Lime and Chilli
"Butter" (see page 178),
to serve

Very simple and very yummy, these pair perfectly with our spicy Memphis Bourbon Barbecue Skewers (*see* page 112). Baby sweet potatoes are becoming more widely available, but if you can't find them, just choose the smallest sweet potatoes you can find. We top them with our fresh, zesty Lime and Chilli "Butter" (*see* page 178).

1   Preheat the oven to 200°C (400°F), Gas Mark 6.

2   Wash the potatoes and remove any rough ends, then pat dry. Make a few incisions into the centre of each potato with a small sharp knife.

3   Rub with the olive oil and sea salt.

4   Cut a piece of foil large enough to wrap the potatoes and an equally large piece of baking parchment. Place the foil on a baking tray and top with the baking parchment. Put all the potatoes on top and then wrap the parchment and foil around the potatoes to seal tightly.

5   Bake for 1–1¼ hours or until the sweet potatoes are becoming soft to the touch.

6   To serve, making a small cut down the length of each potato and squeeze the ends inwards slightly to open up the cut, then top with a spoonful of the lime and chilli "butter".

LEVANT–SPICED BARBECUE CAULIFLOWER

This dish has lots of components and so takes a little time to prepare, but it makes a great colourful addition to any barbecue and is full of flavour, spiked with a typical Middle Eastern blend of spices and finished with a drizzle of creamy tahini sauce and sour pomegranate molasses.

1   Bring a large saucepan of water to the boil, add the cauliflower wedges and cook for about 3-4 minutes until about three-quarters cooked but still firm and holding their shape. Drain and leave to cool under cold running water. Drain and pat dry, then cut into 8 smaller wedges. Put in a bowl and set aside.

2   To make the spice mix, heat the oil in a small saucepan, add the garlic and spices and cook gently for a couple of minutes, stirring, until the spices release their aroma. Add the margarine with the salt and melt over a low heat, then remove from the heat and stir in the lemon juice.

3   Pour the spice mix over the cauliflower and use your hands to rub the mixture into the cauliflower wedges, coating them evenly. Cover and leave to marinate in the refrigerator preferably overnight or for at least a few hours.

4   To make the tahini sauce, put all the ingredients in a bowl and whisk together with a balloon whisk until smooth. Leave to cool – as it does so, the tahini will set and the sauce will thicken slightly. If the sauce thickens too much, whisk in another splash of water to thin it out until it has a pouring consistency.

5   To finish the cauliflower, cook on a hot barbecue or griddle pan on the hob for a few minutes on each side until the wedges are nicely chargrill marked. Serve scattered with the pine nuts, rose petals, pomegranate seeds, parsley and sea salt, and drizzled with the oil, tahini sauce and pomegranate molasses.

SERVES 4-6

1 cauliflower (about 700g/ 1lb 9oz), some inner leaves retained, cut into 4 wedges

FOR THE LEVANT SPICE MIX
2 tablespoons light olive oil
1 large garlic clove, crushed
1 teaspoon sumac
seeds from 3 green cardamom pods, ground
½ teaspoon ground cumin
¼ teaspoon ground cinnamon
¼ teaspoon ground allspice
⅛ teaspoon ground nutmeg
30g (1oz) vegan margarine
¼ teaspoon salt
juice of ½ lemon

FOR THE TAHINI SAUCE
2 tablespoons tahini
juice of 1 lemon
¼ teaspoon salt
½ garlic clove, crushed
100ml (3½fl oz) warm water

TO GARNISH
30g (1oz) pine nuts, toasted
1 tablespoon dried rose petals
seeds from ¼ pomegranate (see page 162)
10g (¼oz) flat leaf parsley, chopped
pinch of sea salt flakes
2 tablespoons olive oil
1 tablespoon pomegranate molasses

GRILLED COURGETTES
WITH ALMOND & PINE NUT PESTO

This pesto makes an ideal accompaniment to the grilled courgettes along with our Soya Labneh (*see* page 246) – and this is a great gluten-free option – but it's equally great served on its own with some grilled Turkish bread as a starter or side dish. Preparing the ingredients by hand will give you a more chunky, rustic pesto.

1 For the pesto, mix all the ingredients together in a bowl until well combined, then set aside.

2 Slice the courgettes on the diagonal about 2cm (¾ inch) thick. Cook on a hot barbecue or griddle pan on the hob for about a minute on each side until nicely chargrill marked.

3 Serve the grilled courgettes with the soya labneh and Turkish bread, topped with plenty of the pesto, and drizzled with some extra virgin olive oil.

SERVES 4-6

2 large courgettes

FOR THE ALMOND AND
  PINE NUT PESTO
60g (2¼oz) Kalamata olives,
  pitted and roughly chopped
1 small red onion, finely diced
30g (1oz) toasted almonds,
  crushed
20g (¾oz) toasted pine nuts,
  crushed
1 large garlic clove, very finely
  chopped
30g (1oz) flat leaf parsley,
  chopped
1½ teaspoons chopped
  oregano leaves
finely chopped zest of 1 lemon
¼ teaspoon chilli flakes
500ml (18fl oz) light olive oil

TO SERVE
Soya Labneh (*see* page 246)
crusty Turkish bread
extra virgin olive oil

GRILLED RAINBOW CHARD
WITH HAZELNUT & ALMOND DUKKAH
& TAHINI SAUCE

SERVES 4–6

600g (1lb 5oz) rainbow chard

splash of olive oil

1 red chilli, thinly sliced

200ml (7fl oz) Tahini Sauce
   (*see* page 144)

2–3 tablespoons Hazelnut
   and Almond Dukkah
   (*see* page 196)

sea salt flakes

lemon wedges, to serve

Rainbow chard has to be one of the most beautiful vegetables, and chargrilling it deepens its fabulous colours as well as drawing out and caramelizing its natural sweetness. The dukkah adds a wonderful spicy crunch to these simple grilled leaves. If you can't get rainbow chard, this approach works equally well with cavolo nero (black kale) or spring greens.

This makes a great side for a barbecue or a Middle Eastern meal, pairing very well with Pistachio and Almond Feta Kibbeh (*see* pages 44–5) or Seitan Lahmajuns (*see* pages 49–51).

1   Wash and drain the chard, then trim the ends of the stems. In a large bowl, toss with the olive oil and the chilli slices and season with sea salt.

2   Heat up a griddle pan or your barbecue to an even medium heat. Spread the chard leaves across the surface of the griddle pan or barbecue rack and cook for about 1–2 minutes on each side until cooked and nicely chargrill marked. If you have to work in batches, keep the cooked chard warm in a dish with a plate on top.

3   Cut the chard leaves in half or, if they are very long, into thirds. Arrange on a serving dish and drizzle with plenty of tahini sauce and then sprinkle with the dukkah. If the chard is in more than one layer, repeat for every layer to ensure the sauce is evenly distributed. Serve with lemon wedges.

ROAST BRUSSELS SPROUTS
WITH SMOKY MAPLE CHESTNUTS

We love a good Brussels sprout, especially a roast one, as the roasting process maximizes its inherent sweetness. We recommend using our herb oil for this recipe, as it will boost the flavour. The smoky maple chestnuts give this side dish a cosy wintery feel. Serve with the Butternut Squash and Tofu Terrine (see pages 100–1) for a special festive meal.

1 Preheat the oven to 190°C (375°F), Gas Mark 5.
2 Wash and drain the sprouts, then trim the bases and remove any thick or damaged outer leaves.
3 In a large bowl, toss the sprouts in the herb oil, sea salt and sage, then spread out in a small roasting tray.
4 Roast for about 20 minutes until the sprouts begin to brown on the outside a little. Add the chestnuts and roast for a further 5 minutes.
5 Remove from the oven, toss with the chopped parsley and serve.

SERVES 4–6

1kg (2lb 4oz) Brussels sprouts
50ml (2fl oz) Herb Oil (see page 186) or 50ml (2fl oz) olive oil mixed with 2 garlic cloves, grated, and $\frac{1}{3}$ teaspoon chopped thyme leaves
large pinch of sea salt flakes
5 sage leaves, cut into strips
200g (7oz) Smoky Maple Chestnuts (see page 177)
5 sprigs of flat leaf parsley, leaves picked and chopped

SERVES 4-6

700g (1lb 9oz) peeled roasting
potatoes (such as Rooster,
Desiree or Maris Piper), cut
into quarters or large chunks

½ teaspoon salt

50ml (2fl oz) light olive oil

3 sprigs of rosemary, leaves
picked

1 whole garlic bulb with skin
on, cut in half horizontally

TO FINISH

20g (¾oz) flat leaf parsley,
chopped

3–4 tablespoons truffle oil

sea salt flakes

The truffle oil in this recipe brings a dash of luxury to the simple roast spuds, making them perfect for celebratory meals. Also, the flat leaf parsley really freshens up the flavours.

Truffle oils vary hugely in strength, so proceed with caution, adding more or less according to taste.

1 Preheat the oven to 200°C (400°F), Gas Mark 6 and put an oven tray in the oven to heat up.

2 Put the potatoes in a large saucepan with enough water to cover and the salt, bring to the boil and parboil for 7-8 minutes. Drain in a colander and leave to air-dry. Toss the potatoes about in the colander to rough them up slightly so that they absorb some of the oil while roasting.

3 Put the potatoes in a bowl with the oil, rosemary and garlic and toss to combine, making sure they are coated evenly in the oil and herbs.

4 Remove the hot baking tray from oven and spread the potatoes out evenly on the tray. Roast for 25-30 minutes until golden, crispy and fully cooked.

5 Remove from the oven and return the potatoes to the bowl. Add the chopped parsley, sprinkle with sea salt flakes and drizzle with the truffle oil. Toss until well combined and serve.

ROAST PUMPKIN
WITH SAVOURY SAGE & PUMPKIN SEED GRANOLA

Since cooking with pumpkin and squash looms large in the USA's national cuisine, Americans are well acquainted with the strange hinterland in which the pumpkin and squash reside, somewhere between sweet and savoury. Europeans, meanwhile, used to balk at pumpkin pie one minute and pumpkin risotto the next, but we are adjusting. Although we draw the line at serving squash or sweet potato with marshmallows, we think you'll enjoy the combination of sweet and savoury in this winter side dish, perfect for serving with a vegan roast or for a holiday meal. Alternatively, this could easily be bumped up to a salad dish in its own right by adding some peppery leaves. Use gluten-free oats for a gluten-free option.

1   To make the granola, preheat the oven to 170°C (340°F), Gas Mark 3½. Line a baking sheet with baking parchment.

2   Mix the oats, pumpkin seeds, sea salt and herbs together in a bowl. Measure out the oil, maple syrup and chilli jam into a jug and whisk with a fork to combine. Add to the oat mixture and mix together well.

3   Turn the granola mixture out on to the lined baking sheet and bake for 15–20 minutes, stirring occasionally, until it begins to brown. Remove from the oven and leave to cool.

4   To roast the pumpkin, preheat the oven to 200°C (400°F), Gas Mark 6. Line a roasting tray with baking parchment.

5   Toss the pumpkin or squash wedges with the oil, sea salt and sage in a bowl. Turn out on to the lined roasting tray and roast for 45 minutes–1 hour until cooked through but still holding their shape.

6   Crumble the granola over the warm pumpkin or squash and serve.

SERVES 6–8, DEPENDING ON THE SIZE OF THE PUMPKIN/SQUASH

FOR THE GRANOLA

50g (1¾oz) jumbo oats

25g (1oz) pumpkin seeds

½ tablespoon sea salt flakes

4 sage leaves, roughly chopped

½ teaspoon roughly chopped thyme leaves

3 tablespoons olive oil

4 teaspoons maple syrup

1 tablespoon Smoked Chilli Jam (*see* page 180) or 1 tablespoon redcurrant jelly and a large pinch of smoked paprika and chilli flakes

FOR THE PUMPKIN

I small pumpkin or butternut squash, deseeded and cut into wedges 2cm (¾ inch) wide

50ml (2fl oz) light olive oil

½ teaspoon sea salt flakes

6 sage leaves

TARRAGON RANCH POTATO SALAD

Our homemade ranch dip makes a delicious dressing for this simple summer potato salad. The fresh tarragon and sweetness of the cooked shallots perfectly offset the creamy dressing, making a lovely quick side dish for a lunch outdoors or a barbecue. Try this with our tangy Memphis Bourbon Barbecue Skewers (see page 112).

1   Wash the potatoes in plenty of cold water, then put them in a saucepan with enough water to cover and the salt. Bring to the boil, then cover and simmer for about 15-20 minutes until they are fully cooked and beginning to break apart when prodded. Drain in a colander and leave to air-dry and cool slightly.

2   Heat the oil in a small frying pan, add the shallots and fry over a medium heat for 6-8 minutes until they are golden, adding the chopped tarragon at the last minute, stirring constantly.

3   Transfer the shallots and tarragon to a bowl with the potatoes, sea salt, cracked pink pepper, ranch dip and soya cream and toss together until well combined. Check the seasoning and serve.

SERVES 4-6

750g (1lb 10oz) new potatoes, cut in half or into medium-sized chunks

½ teaspoon salt

splash of light oil (groundnut or sunflower)

3 shallots, thinly sliced

10g (¼oz) tarragon, chopped

1 teaspoon sea salt flakes

¼ teaspoon cracked pink pepper

3 tablespoons Ranch Dip (see page 174)

3 tablespoons soya cream

SAUTÉED DILL GREENS

SERVES 4

500g (1lb 2oz) cabbage or
   spring greens
1 tablespoon light olive oil
15g (½oz) vegan margarine
100g (3½oz) peas (defrosted
   if frozen)
¼ teaspoon salt
20g (¾oz) dill, chopped

This is another Polish-inspired dish and another versatile side, great served with Smoked Tofu and White Bean Sausages (*see* page 81) and Creamy Mustard Mash (*see* page 164) or as part of a barbecue spread.

1   Remove and discard the outer leaves from the cabbage or spring greens, then cut in half, core, and dice into 5cm (2-inch) cubes. Wash and drain.

2   Heat the oil in a deep frying pan or saucepan over a medium-high heat to just about smoking point. Toss the greens into the pan and cook for 2-3 minutes, stirring constantly, until they have softened slightly but are still crunchy and are slightly browned.

3   Add the vegan margarine, peas and salt and cook for a further minute, stirring, to heat the peas through and combine everything well. Remove from the hob, mix in the chopped dill and serve.

MISO-GLAZED AUBERGINE

This sweet and salty Japanese classic, called *nasu dengaku*, is super-easy to prepare and makes a distinctive side dish, or try it as an alternative component of the Tokyo Bowl (*see* pages 118–21). Alternatively, turn it into a main event by serving it with a fresh mango and soba noodle salad. Use gluten-free miso and tamari for a gluten-free option.

1 Preheat the oven to 200°C (400°F), Gas Mark 6.
2 Cut the aubergines in half lengthways and score the cut sides in a cross-cross pattern, cutting almost all the way down through the flesh but without piercing the skin.
3 Heat a griddle pan or cast-iron frying pan over a medium-high heat. Brush both sides of the aubergines with the blended oil, making sure you give the cut sides of the aubergine a generous coating so that the oil is absorbed into the flesh.
4 Cook the aubergines for about 2 minutes on each side to char them slightly. Transfer them to a baking tray, cut side up, and bake for 20–25 minutes until the flesh is fully cooked and soft.
5 While the aubergines are cooking, prepare your garnish. Cut the spring onion into 3–4 batons, slice in half and then finely slice them lengthways. Add them to a bowl of chilled water and refrigerate until ready to serve.
6 To make the glaze, heat the miso, tamari or soy sauce, mirin and sugar in a small saucepan, bring to a simmer and whisk well to form a smooth paste. Cook for 3–4 minutes, adding the ginger at the last minute. Remove from the heat and set aside.
7 Remove the aubergines from the oven and brush the tops generously with the glaze, letting it seep into the flesh. Increase the oven temperature to 240°C (475°F), Gas Mark 9 or heat the grill to a high heat. Cook the aubergines for a further 3–5 minutes until the glaze begins to bubble and caramelize slightly.
8 Drain the finely sliced spring onions and use to garnish the aubergines, along with the sesame seeds, before serving.

SERVES 4

2 aubergines
2 tablespoons blended oil (half vegetable and half sesame)

FOR THE GLAZE

1½ tablespoons red or white miso
½ tablespoon tamari (gluten-free) or soy sauce
100ml (3½fl oz) mirin
½ tablespoon caster sugar
1 teaspoon finely grated fresh root ginger

TO GARNISH

1 spring onion
1 teaspoon toasted black or white sesame seeds

SAUTÉED SPINACH
WITH GOLDEN SULTANAS & SALTED PISTACHIOS

We love the beautiful colour in this simple Middle Eastern side dish, and it illustrates why we find it baffling that the stems of spinach are often discarded when they are so tender and delicious. If you can't find golden sultanas, you can use regular sultanas or raisins. You can buy ready-prepared salted shelled pistachios, but if you can't get hold of them, salting your own is pretty simple (*see* page 57).

Try serving this with our Butternut Squash and Pistachio Borek (*see* page 52) or Pistachio and Almond Feta Kibbeh (*see* pages 44-5).

1   Soak the sultanas in the measured warm water and lemon juice for 30 minutes-1 hour.

2   Wash the spinach thoroughly and drain, then trim the ends of the stems and discard any tough bits. Cut the leaves, including the stems, into 2 or 3 pieces depending on their size.

3   Heat a splash of light olive oil in a frying pan, add the spinach and sauté over a medium heat for 3-4 minutes, stirring, until it begins to soften. Remove from the pan and drain in a colander.

4   Add a little more oil to the pan, add the onion and garlic and sauté for 5-10 minutes, stirring frequently, until golden.

5   Drain the sultanas and add to the onion, then return the spinach to the pan and warm through over a medium heat. Season to taste with salt and pepper. Finally, toss in the salted pistachios and then serve.

SERVES 4-6

30g (1oz) golden sultanas
100ml (3½fl oz) warm water
squeeze of lemon juice
500g (1lb 2oz) large leaf
   spinach with stems
light olive oil
1 white onion, very thinly sliced
2 garlic cloves, finely sliced
extra virgin olive oil
60g (2¼oz) salted shelled
   pistachio nuts (*see* page 57
   for homemade)
salt and pepper

WHITE WINE–BRAISED LEEKS & PLUM TOMATOES

SERVES 4-6

2–3 leeks, trimmed and tough
   outer leaves discarded
   (350g/12oz prepared
   weight), washed

6 plum tomatoes, halved and
   stems removed

200ml (7fl oz) dry white wine

100ml (3½fl oz) Light
   Vegetable Stock (*see* page
   251) or water

6 sage leaves

3 sprigs of thyme

1 teaspoon sea salt flakes

3 tablespoons olive oil

2 tablespoons lilliput capers

The braising liquid of this dish is delicious and can be used in place of gravy, so it pairs very well with our Smoked Tofu and White Bean Sausages (*see* page 81) and Creamy Mustard Mash (*see* page 164). It can also be served at room temperature as a starter with loads of warm crusty bread to mop up the juices.

1   Preheat the oven to 190°C (375°F), Gas Mark 5.

2   Cut the leeks into 5cm (2-inch) chunks. Pack closely into an ovenproof dish with the plum tomatoes.

3   Pour over the wine and the stock or water and sprinkle over the herbs, sea salt, olive oil and capers. Cover with foil and bake for 30 minutes until the leeks are quite tender.

4   Remove the leeks from the oven and increase the oven temperature to 220°C (425°F), Gas Mark 7. Lift off the foil and turn the leeks a little, then return to the oven, uncovered, for a further 10-15 minutes until the leeks begin to turn dark golden.

EZME SALAD

The name of this beautiful Turkish salad translates as "crushed salad", and in any of the best Turkish restaurants they will chop all the ingredients for it to order using a two-handled chopper. The pomegranate and tomatoes release loads of liquid, but that's the point, as the dish acts as part salad, part dip and part dressing, and in this sense it's comparable to a traditional Mexican salsa. A fantastic scarlet and purple colour, this salad is wonderful with Pistachio and Almond Feta Kibbeh (*see* pages 44-5), Butternut Squash and Pistachio Borek (*see* page 52) and Seitan Lahmajuns (*see* pages 49-51), as well as all things barbecued or grilled.

Deseeding a pomegranate is great for unleashing a little controlled aggression, but just don't wear a white top while you're doing it. Place a large bowl in the sink, then cut the pomegranate in half over it. Hold a pomegranate half, cut side down, in one hand over the bowl and a rolling pin or similar blunt instrument in the other hand and whack the skin side until all the seeds have come out. Pick out the white bits and you're ready to go. Alternatively, pomegranate seeds are now quite widely available to buy.

1 Very finely dice the tomato, red pepper, onion and red chilli.
2 Put in a bowl with all the remaining ingredients and mix together with your hands, crushing the ingredients slightly as you do so.
3 We like to leave the salad to rest for at least 30 minutes before serving, at cool room temperature or in the refrigerator, to release the flavours.

SERVES 4-6

2 small or 1 large ripe tomato, quartered and deseeded

½ red pepper, cored and deseeded

½ red onion

½ red chilli, deseeded

seeds of ½ pomegranate (about 80g/3oz)

1 garlic clove, crushed or finely chopped

1-2 tablespoons pomegranate molasses

½ tablespoon sumac

2 tablespoons olive oil

2 tablespoons lemon juice

pinch of chilli powder

30g (1oz) flat leaf parsley, finely chopped

salt

CREAMY MUSTARD MASH

We serve this creamy mash with our Smoked Tofu and White Bean Sausages (*see* page 81). The mustard gives it a pleasant tang, but if you're not keen on its flavour, simply leave it out.

1   Wash the potatoes in plenty of cold water and drain, then put them in a large saucepan with enough water to cover and some salt. Bring to the boil and then cover and simmer for 25-30 minutes until soft but not totally falling apart.

2   In a separate saucepan, warm the plant-based milk and cream with the garlic and vegan margarine, stirring occasionally to stop the garlic sticking on the base of the pan.

3   When the potatoes are cooked, drain them and then immediately mash with a potato masher or a balloon whisk. Strain the warm milk mixture, to remove the garlic, into the potatoes and whisk it in until fluffy.

4   Add the mustard and enough plant-based crème fraîche to achieve a really smooth consistency. It will be warm enough to eat immediately, but should you need to reheat it, make sure you stir gently and frequently as you do so - you may need to add more cream.

SERVES 4-6

1kg (2lb 4oz) Maris Piper potatoes, peeled and halved or quartered

200ml (7fl oz) unsweetened plant-based milk

125ml (4fl oz) plant-based cream (such as oat or soya)

2 garlic cloves, sliced

30g (1oz) vegan margarine

2 teaspoons grain mustard

about 125ml (4fl oz) plant-based crème fraîche

salt and pepper

CORNBREAD

SERVES 4–6

100g (3½oz) sweetcorn kernels

200g (7oz) polenta

100g (3½oz) plain flour

3 teaspoons baking powder

3 tablespoons sugar

1 teaspoon salt

3 tablespoons vegetarian
   suet or fat

3 tablespoons nutritional
   yeast flakes

200ml (7fl oz) soya yogurt

200ml (7fl oz) soya milk

1 red chilli, diced (optional)

Delicious with just about everything, for breakfast, brunch or a summer barbecue, this recipe is quick and easy to make.

1   Preheat the oven to 200°C (400°F), Gas Mark 6. Line a small baking tray, about 15cm (6 inches) square and 5cm (2 inches) deep, or a 15cm (6-inch) round cake tin with baking parchment.

2   Put the sweetcorn kernels in a blender and blitz to a purée.

3   Add all the dry ingredients to a bowl and mix together well. Add the puréed corn with all the remaining ingredients and use either a balloon whisk or hand-held electric whisk to whisk everything together until well combined.

4   Pour the mixture into the lined baking tray or cake tin and bake for 25–30 minutes until the bread has risen and begun to colour. To check if it's cooked, a metal skewer inserted into centre should come out clean, but if dough is stuck to it, bake for a further 5 minutes and check again.

5   Turn out on to a wire rack and leave to rest for 15–20 minutes before serving.

ACCOMPANIMENTS

PINEAPPLE SALSA

This vibrant salsa is equally delicious prepared either using the barbecue or a griddle pan on the hob, and is highly versatile as a condiment or side dish. Serve it with tortilla chips for dipping, or to accompany the Spiced Black Beans as an alternative component of the Puebla Bowl (*see* pages 122-5).

1   Remove the skin and core from the pineapple and slice the flesh about 2cm (¾ inch) thick.
2   Heat a barbecue or griddle pan to a high heat, add the pineapple slices and cook for 3-4 minutes on each side until they have charred slightly. Remove from the heat and leave to cool.
3   Add the remaining ingredients to a bowl. Dice the grilled pineapple into 1cm (½-inch) cubes, add to the bowl and mix well. Check for seasoning and then serve.

SERVES 4-6

½ pineapple (400g/14oz)
1 red chilli, deseeded and diced
20g (¾oz) coriander, chopped
½ red onion, finely diced
1 teaspoon sugar
pinch of salt

BASIL PESTO

Basil pesto is such a crowd-pleaser and a favourite with a lot of children. Serve as a simple main with pasta, trofie in particular, or with grilled vegetables or crispy polenta (*see* page 56). The nutritional yeast imitates the flavour of the traditional Parmesan cheese in this otherwise classic pesto.

1   Put all the ingredients, except the pine nuts, in a food processor, or use a stick blender fitted with the chopping/drum attachment, and pulse until you have a chunky paste. Then add the pine nuts and pulse a couple more times.

2   Alternatively, chop the basil, garlic and pine nuts very finely by hand. Put in a bowl with the remaining ingredients and mash together with the end of a rolling pin or similar blunt instrument.

3   Store in a clean airtight jar or container in the refrigerator - it will keep for up to a week or so. It can also be frozen.

MAKES 8-10 SERVINGS

150g (5½oz) sprigs of basil,
  leaves picked
1 large garlic clove, peeled
2 tablespoons nutritional
  yeast flakes
grated zest of 1 lemon
90g (3¼oz) pine nuts, toasted
100ml (3½fl oz) light oil (such
  as sunflower, rapeseed or
  light olive oil)
salt and pepper

RED PESTO

MAKES 8–10 SERVINGS

200g (7oz) piquillo peppers
   from a jar, drained and
   roughly chopped

100g (3½oz) sun-blushed
   tomatoes, drained (oil
   reserved) and roughly
   chopped

100ml (3½fl oz) oil reserved
   from the sun-blushed
   tomatoes

3 garlic cloves, peeled

6 slices of red chilli

10g (¼oz) basil leaves,
   sliced or torn

2 tablespoons nutritional
   yeast flakes

grated zest of 1 lemon

pinch of sugar

2 tablespoons tomato purée

60g (2¼oz) pine nuts, toasted

salt and pepper

A vibrant red pesto that, besides being perfect with pasta such as penne or trofie, is also great as a topping for Pides (*see* pages 104-9) or crostini. We use roasted and skinned piquillo peppers available in jars, but you can also use the same quantity of homemade roasted and skinned red peppers (*see* page 180). As with the Basil Pesto (*see* opposite), the nutritional yeast contributes a Parmesan-like flavour.

1   Follow the instructions for Basil Pesto opposite to make; if making without a food processor or stick blender, chop the piquillo peppers, sun-blushed tomatoes, garlic, chilli and pine nuts very finely by hand before mashing together with the remaining ingredients.

2   Store as for the basil pesto opposite.

CARROT, BUTTER BEAN & CARAWAY DIP
WITH HAZELNUT & ALMOND DUKKAH

The brilliant orange of this dip is wonderful and the taste is quite gentle and fragrant. It can be served alone, but we love the combination of this dip with the spice and crunch of our nutty dukkah and some warm grilled flatbread (omit the bread for a gluten-free option).

1 Preheat the oven to 180°C (350°F), Gas Mark 4. Line a baking tray with baking parchment.
2 Toss the carrot slices with a little olive oil, the orange juice and sea salt in a bowl until they are evenly coated. Spread the carrots out on the lined baking tray and roast for about 15–20 minutes until tender. Remove from the oven and leave to cool slightly.
3 Toast the spice seeds in a dry frying pan over a gentle heat for a couple of minutes, stirring, until they release their aroma. Remove from the heat and then grind the spices with a pestle and mortar or an electric spice grinder.
4 Blend all the ingredients, except the dukkah, in a blender, or in a measuring jug with a stick blender, until completely smooth.
5 Transfer to a bowl and top with a little olive oil and then the dukkah.

SERVES 8–10

500g (1lb 2oz) carrots, cut into slices 5mm (¼ inch) thick
juice of ½ orange
large pinch of sea salt flakes
2 teaspoons caraway seeds
½ teaspoon cumin seeds
½ teaspoon coriander seeds
1 garlic clove, peeled
pinch of sugar
75ml (5 tablespoons) olive oil, plus extra for roasting the carrots and to serve
50ml (2fl oz) water
400g (14oz) can butter beans, drained and rinsed
squeeze of lemon juice
2–3 tablespoons Hazelnut and Almond Dukkah (*see page 196*), to serve

BROAD BEAN & MINT DIP

A great dip to make when fresh broad beans are in season, although frozen broad beans can be used at other times. This dip goes well with some slow-roasted cherry tomatoes and crusty bread.

1 Cook the broad beans in a saucepan of lightly salted boiling water for 3–5 minutes, then drain and leave to cool, reserving 150ml (5fl oz) of the cooking water.
2 Peel the broad beans, then blend with the remaining ingredients in a blender, or in a measuring jug with a stick blender, to a purée. Check for seasoning, transfer to a bowl and serve.

SERVES 8–10

500g (1lb 2oz) podded broad beans
1–2 garlic cloves, peeled
7–8 sprigs of mint, leaves picked and chopped (10g/¼oz)
10g (¼oz) flat leaf parsley, chopped
100ml (3½fl oz) light olive oil
salt and white pepper

RANCH DIP

A classic American dip or dressing, ranch is traditionally made with soured cream, which gives it a distinctive tang. Created by one of our talented chefs, Wayne Glass, this vegan version replaces the regular soured cream with soya cream and yogurt, but if you have issues with soya, use oat cream and oat crème fraîche respectively in the same quantities. Ume plum seasoning is a salty sour Japanese sauce that is essentially the pickling juice from traditional umeboshi plum pickles, and provides a little umami kick, although if you can't find it, don't worry as it's not vital.

There is no need to incorporate the oil slowly, as soya products don't split easily. Having said that, if too much oil is added, the mixture *will* split, in which event simply add more soya cream or yogurt and it will return to a smooth emulsion. If you want to use this as a salad dressing, loosen it up with some extra soya cream or soya milk or a little water.

This stars in our Tarragon Ranch Potato Salad (*see* page 156) or use it to dress a salad of iceberg lettuce wedges, or serve with crudités to accompany our Buffalo-marinated Tofu with Crunchy Crumb Coating (*see* page 48) or as a dip with potato wedges.

1   Blend all the ingredients, except the herbs, in a blender, or in a measuring jug with a stick blender, until the mixture thickens.
2   Transfer to a bowl, add the dill and chives and fold through with a spoon or spatula. Check the seasoning.
3   The dip will keep in an airtight container in the refrigerator for up to 6 days.

MAKES 8–10 SERVINGS

100ml (3½fl oz) soya cream
1 teaspoon ume plum seasoning
1 teaspoon Dijon mustard
2 tablespoons lemon juice
1 teaspoon nutritional yeast flakes
½ teaspoon garlic powder
50ml (2fl oz) vegetable oil
50ml (2fl oz) light olive oil
good pinch of salt and white pepper
2 tablespoons soya yogurt
5g (⅛oz) dill, finely chopped
5g (⅛oz) chives, finely chopped

ROAST SUNFLOWER & PUMPKIN SEED HUMMUS

SERVES 8-10

60g (2¼oz) sunflower seeds

250g (9oz) peeled and
deseeded pumpkin or
butternut squash, diced into
2.5cm (1-inch) cubes

3 garlic cloves, peeled

250ml (9fl oz) light olive oil

400g (14oz) can good-quality
chickpeas, drained and
rinsed

½ teaspoon salt

TO GARNISH

toasted pumpkin seeds

sunflower seed sprouts or other
sprouting seeds

This tahini-free hummus is full of autumn character. The taste of the sunflower seeds is somewhat subtler than tahini and gives the hummus a nice nutty flavour, and paired with the slight sweetness of the pumpkin, it's a great take on a classic dip. It's worth seeking out a good roasting pumpkin, rather than a watery Halloween type.

1 Put the sunflower seeds in a heatproof bowl, pour over boiling water to cover and leave to soak for 1-2 hours.

2 Meanwhile, preheat the oven to 200°C (400°F), Gas Mark 6.

3 Toss the pumpkin or squash cubes with the garlic cloves and 2 tablespoons of the oil in a bowl until they are evenly coated with the oil. Spread out on a baking tray and roast for 10-15 minutes until the squash is fully cooked.

4 Remove from the oven and leave to cool. Set aside about 100g (3½oz) of the cooked pumpkin or squash to fold through the dip before serving.

5 Drain the sunflower seeds, add them to a small blender, or to a measuring jug for using a stick blender, and blitz them to a fine paste. Add the remaining ingredients and blend to a smooth consistency. Check the seasoning, transfer to a bowl and fold through the reserved pumpkin or squash.

6 Garnish the dip with toasted pumpkin seeds and sunflower seed sprouts or other sprouting seeds to serve.

COCONUT "BACON"

The smoky sweetness of this coconut is delicious in salads or as a crunchy topping for baked potatoes, and goes especially well with our Ranch Dip (*see* page 174). You will need dried coconut flakes (or shavings) here rather than desiccated coconut.

1 Preheat the oven to 140°C (275°F), Gas Mark 1. Brush a baking tray with the melted coconut oil.

2 Using a small balloon whisk, whisk the tamari or soy sauce, maple syrup, liquid smoke and paprika together in a large bowl, making sure you disperse any clumps of paprika.

3 Add the coconut flakes and salt and gently toss for 45 seconds until each flake is well coated in the tamari/soy mixture.

4 Spread the coconut flakes out in a thin layer on the oiled baking tray so that they toast evenly. Toast in the oven for 15–20 minutes, stirring occasionally, until the coconut has dried and begun to brown slightly.

5 Remove from the oven and leave to cool. Store in an airtight container in a cool, dry place. It will keep well for weeks.

MAKES 6–8 SERVINGS

1 tablespoon melted coconut oil (or any light oil), for oiling

1 tablespoon tamari (gluten-free) or soy sauce

1 tablespoon maple syrup

1 teaspoon liquid smoke (*see* page 31)

¼ teaspoon sweet paprika

100g (3½oz) coconut flakes

pinch of salt

SMOKY MAPLE CHESTNUTS

MAKES 6-8 SERVINGS

1 tablespoon olive oil, for oiling

1 tablespoon tamari (gluten-
    free) or soy sauce

1 tablespoon maple syrup

1 teaspoon liquid smoke
    (*see* page 31)

¼ teaspoon sweet paprika

250g (9oz) cooked peeled
    chestnuts

1 tablespoon gluten-free plain
    flour or rice flour or cornflour

pinch of salt

These chestnuts are excellent with Roast Pumpkin (*see* page 154) or Roast Brussels Sprouts (*see* page 150). They can also be eaten as a wintery snack.

1   Preheat the oven to 170°C (340°F), Gas Mark 3½. Brush a baking tray with the olive oil.

2   Using a small balloon whisk, whisk the tamari or soy sauce, maple syrup, liquid smoke and paprika together in a small bowl, making sure you disperse any clumps of paprika.

3   Put the chestnuts in a large bowl with the flour and salt and toss together. Add the tamari/soy mixture and toss again until each chestnut is well coated.

4   Spread out in a thin layer on the baking tray so that the chestnuts roast evenly. Roast in the oven for 15-20 minutes, stirring occasionally.

5   Remove from the oven and leave to cool. Store in an airtight container in a cool, dry place. They will keep well for weeks.

LIME & CHILLI "BUTTER"

Keeping a bowl of this on hand during a barbecue to add to grilled vegetables or to smear across freshly grilled flatbreads will instantly elevate their flavours. The freshness of the lime and chilli is a great foil to the intensity of chargrilled food.

Simple to make, the "butter" keeps well in the refrigerator, but you can also shape it into a log with a sheet of clingfilm or baking parchment, then wrap the log up and twist the ends to seal. Freeze the roll and slice off rounds as needed.

1 Put all the ingredients in a food processor and blend until combined.
2 Alternatively, leave the margarine out of the refrigerator to soften slightly and then place in a bowl with all the remaining ingredients and whisk vigorously with a balloon whisk or hand-held electric whisk.
3 Store in an airtight container in the refrigerator for up to a week or freeze as above.

MAKES 8–10 SERVINGS

250g (9oz) soya margarine
50ml (2fl oz) olive oil
50ml (2fl oz) soya cream
100g (3½oz) coriander, chopped
1 red chilli, chopped
grated zest and juice of 2 limes
4 garlic cloves, grated
1 teaspoon sea salt flakes

SMOKED CHILLI JAM

We use this sweet smoky condiment both as an ingredient and as a dressing (*see* photo, page 179). It adds a real depth of flavour to our Savoury Sage and Pumpkin Seed Granola (*see* page 154) and glazes, and can be thinned with a little water or orange juice and used to marinate tofu or tempeh before cooking. It pairs wonderfully with any chargrilled vegetables but especially peppers and leeks (*see* page 56). If you cook up a big batch and jar it up nicely, it makes a great gift too.

1 Start by roasting or charring your red pepper, either in a hot oven, on the hob over a gas flame or on the barbecue.

2 If using the oven method, preheat to 240°C (475°F), Gas Mark 9. Rub the red pepper lightly with oil, sit on a baking tray and roast for about 15-20 minutes, turning frequently, until the skin is blistered on all sides.

3 Alternatively, place the pepper directly on a gas burner of the hob turned to high, turning frequently with tongs, until the skin blisters, or do the same over a hot barbecue.

4 Transfer the red pepper to a bowl, cover with clingfilm and leave to cool, then peel off the skin and remove the stem, core and seeds.

5 Blend the red pepper and chipotle chilli with the measured water in small blender, or in a measuring jug with a stick blender, to a purée. Add the purée to a saucepan with all the remaining ingredients and bring to a simmer, giving the mixture a whisk with a balloon whisk every so often to make sure the agar agar dissolves into the liquid.

6 Simmer the jam for 15-20 minutes, then remove from the heat and leave to cool. It should thicken up while cooling until it resembles a firm jelly. Once cool, spoon into clean airtight jars or bottles and store in the refrigerator for 2-3 weeks.

MAKES 10-15 SERVINGS

1 red pepper
light oil (such as sunflower, groundnut or light olive oil)
1 chipotle chilli in adobo sauce
500ml (18fl oz) water
350g (12oz) demerara sugar
grated zest and juice of ½ lemon
2½ tablespoons agar agar flakes
½ teaspoon chilli flakes
¼ teaspoon liquid smoke (*see* page 31)
½ teaspoon salt

ROAST GARLIC AIOLI

MAKES 8-10 SERVINGS

8-12 garlic cloves, depending
  on size, peeled
50ml (2fl oz) light olive oil
¼ teaspoon sea salt flakes

FOR THE MAYO
150ml (5fl oz) good-quality
  unsweetened soya milk
200ml (7fl oz) light oil (such
  as sunflower or rapeseed)
2 tablespoons orange juice
2 tablespoons lemon juice
salt and pepper

The garlic in this aioli is confit in olive oil and is therefore quite mellow, which makes this a great base mayonnaise to which you can add other ingredients, while still being really tasty in itself (*see* photograph overleaf). The amazing thing about making vegan mayonnaise is that, unlike its eggy older cousin, you don't have the faff of having to drizzle the oil in carefully. Just add it all in one go and blend, and if it splits a little or is too thick, just mix in a little more plant milk, or if too thin, add a dash more oil. Easy peasy.

1   Preheat the oven to 180°C (350°F), Gas Mark 4.
2   Put the garlic cloves in a small baking tray or ovenproof frying pan, drizzle with the oil and sprinkle with the sea salt. Cover with a sheet of foil or baking parchment and bake for 20-30 minutes, stirring halfway through, until the garlic is soft and has begun to colour. Remove from the oven and leave to cool to room temperature.
3   Blend all the mayo ingredients with the roast garlic in a blender, or in a measuring jug with a stick blender, until well combined. Add a little more soya milk if it's too thick or oil if it's too thin, and taste and adjust the seasoning.
4   Store in a clean airtight jar or other container in the refrigerator. It will keep for at least 2 weeks.

WASABI MAYO

MAKES 8-10 SERVINGS

200g (7oz) Roast Garlic Aioli
  (*see* above)
45g (1½oz) wasabi paste,
  or to taste
grated zest and juice of 1 lime
½ tablespoon agave syrup (or
  other mild-flavoured syrup)

The quantity of wasabi specified here gives you a fairly mild kick, but it's really down to your personal taste, so feel free to add more if you're hardcore. If you have the powdered kind of wasabi instead of the pre-mixed, just add enough water or lime juice to form a paste before adding it to the aioli (*see* photograph overleaf).

1   Mix all the ingredients together in a bowl until well combined. Taste and adjust the seasoning and wasabi heat factor as desired. Store as for the Roast Garlic Aioli (*see* above).

VEGAN CAESAR DRESSING

Nutritional yeast gives a cheesy tang to this super-easy vegan Caesar dressing. Our Caesar salad practically flies off the salad bar at our Soho branch.

1 Put all the ingredients in a measuring jug and blend with a stick blender until smooth. If it looks too thick or like it may have split, add a splash more soya cream or soya milk.

2 Alternatively, put all the ingredients, except the oil, in a bowl. Whisk vigorously with a balloon whisk and then, continuing to whisk constantly, add the oil in a slow, steady stream (it helps if you can get someone else to do the pouring) until all incorporated.

3 Store in a clean airtight jar in the refrigerator. It will keep for well over a week.

MAKES ABOUT 500ML (18FL OZ)

250ml (9fl oz) soya cream or soya milk

1 large or 2 small garlic cloves, peeled

juice of 1 lemon

1 tablespoon Henderson's Relish (*see* page 28)

1 tablespoon nutritional yeast flakes

½ teaspoon Tabasco sauce

1 teaspoon Dijon mustard

pinch of ground cayenne

pinch of ground white pepper

150ml (5fl oz) light oil (such as sunflower or rapeseed)

MOJO DE AJO

MAKES 8-10 SERVINGS

20-30 garlic cloves,
   depending on size, peeled
100ml (3½fl oz) extra virgin
   olive oil
¼ teaspoon sea salt flakes
1 teaspoon oregano leaves,
   finely chopped
large pinch of Arbol chilli
   flakes
75ml (5 tablespoons) orange
   juice (from about 2 oranges)
50ml (2fl oz) lime juice (from
   about 1½ limes)

Don't be scared of the huge quantity of garlic in this sauce, as the slow cooking and the citrus juices mellow and sweeten the garlic. Somewhere between a sauce and a condiment, this can be eaten hot or at room temperature. We've served it with the Roast Tenderstem Broccoli (*see* page 142) and it's also good with our Grilled Rainbow Chard (*see* page 148), but you can even just scoop it up with some warm bread.

1   Preheat the oven to 180°C (350°F), Gas Mark 4.
2   Put the garlic cloves in a small baking tray or ovenproof frying pan, drizzle with the oil and sprinkle with the sea salt, oregano and chilli flakes. Cover with a sheet of foil or baking parchment and bake for 45 minutes, stirring halfway through.
3   Add the citrus juices, re-cover and bake for a further 15 minutes.
4   Remove from the oven. At this stage, you can either transfer to a bowl and mash with a fork to achieve a thick paste or, for a smoother finish, pulse a little in a food processor or with a stick blender fitted with the chopping/drum attachment.
5   Store in a clean airtight jar or other airtight container in the refrigerator. It will keep for up to a couple of weeks.

ORANGE, MAPLE & THYME DRESSING

We use this dressing for the Rainbow Root Slaw (*see* page 140), as the mixture of sweet citrus and earthy thyme is particularly good with roasted root vegetables or in salads. It's a great dressing for wedges of roast pumpkin or squash, and can be added before or after roasting. It also makes a nice glaze for nuts when added before roasting, especially pecans.

1   Blend all the ingredients in a blender, or in a measuring jug with a stick blender, until smooth and glossy.
2   Transfer to a clean large airtight jar or bottle.
3   Alternatively, very finely chop the garlic and thyme by hand. Put in the jar or bottle with the remaining ingredients, seal and shake vigorously until well combined.
4   Store in the refrigerator for up to 2 weeks.

MAKES 10–12 SERVINGS

4 garlic cloves, peeled
4 sprigs of thyme, leaves picked
grated zest of 1 orange
250ml (9fl oz) olive oil
200ml (7fl oz) orange juice
100ml (3½fl oz) maple syrup
salt and pepper

HERB OIL

This is such a useful oil to have in the refrigerator ready to boost the flavour of simple roast vegetables or potato wedges.

1   Blend all the ingredients in a blender, or in a measuring jug with a stick blender, until the herbs are broken down into small pieces.
2   Transfer to a clean lar   airtight jar or bottle.
3   Alternatively   hop the garlic and herbs by hand. Put in the   oil and salt to taste, seal and shake
    d.
    to 2 weeks.

MAKES 10–12 SERVINGS

4–6 garlic cloves, peeled
3 sprigs of rosemary,
   leaves picked
3 sprigs of thyme, leaves picked
500ml (18fl oz) light oil (such
   as sunflower or rapeseed)
salt

PERSIAN LIME & ROSE HARISSA

MAKES 8–10 SERVINGS

4–6 red Romano peppers
(500g/1lb 2oz total weight)

5 red chillies (70g/2½oz
total weight)

1 teaspoon cumin seeds

1 teaspoon coriander seeds

2 teaspoon Arbol chilli flakes

1 Persian lime, soaked (*see
recipe introduction*), then
drained and deseeded

2 garlic cloves, peeled

3 tablespoons rose petals,
fresh or dried

1 tablespoon sweet paprika

100ml (3½fl oz) light olive oil,
plus extra for rubbing the
peppers and chillies

This versatile ingredient (*see* photograph overleaf) is great for adding an extra dimension of flavour to Middle Eastern-inspired dishes such as couscous or freekeh, and it features in our Persian Lime and Chickpea Stew (*see* page 92).

Rose is one of those "Marmite flavours" in that some people love it while other people think it tastes like potpourri – we're firmly in the love it camp. The rose note in this harissa is subtle, but if you're really keen on the flavour, you can boost it by adding a couple of drops of rosewater. If you can get fresh edible rose petals, they really will elevate the flavour of this harissa. However, for the haters out there, if you want to make a simple red pepper harissa, just omit the rose and lime.

The Persian lime is a small dried lime with a distinctive sour fragrant flavour, which lends a citrus undertone to this spicy paste. As the limes come dried, they need to be soaked for a few hours in hot water before using. If you can't find them, the nearest ingredient is preserved lemon. I'm using Romano peppers for this recipe because they cook quickly and are easy to peel, but you can use regular red peppers or roasted and skinned jarred peppers if you wish.

1   Preheat the oven to 240°C (475°F), Gas Mark 9.

2   Rub a little oil over the peppers and chillies, spread them out on a baking tray and roast for 10–15 minutes, turning frequently, until the skin is blistered on all sides.

3   Remove from the oven, then transfer to a bowl, cover with clingfilm and leave to cool. As soon as they are cool enough to handle, peel off the skins and remove the stems and seeds.

4   Meanwhile, toast the cumin and coriander seeds and chilli flakes in a dry frying pan over a gentle heat for 2–3 minutes, stirring, until they release their aroma. Remove from the heat and then grind the spices with a pestle and mortar or an electric spice grinder.

5   Put the roasted peppers and chillies and the toasted spices with all the remaining ingredients in a food processor, or use a stick blender fitted with the chopping/drum attachment, and pulse until you achieve the desired consistency. We favour a chunky paste.

6   Store in a clean airtight jar in the refrigerator. It will keep for up to a couple of weeks.

HOME PICKLING

Home pickling is good fun, from the preparation to watching it ferment and finally tasting the final product. It's one of the oldest methods of preserving food and it's fairly easy to do. Home-fermented foods are also packed with beneficial natural probiotics and vitamins. The simple, classic pickling recipes in this book provide a great introduction to basic pickling.

FERMENTING TIPS

* Make sure any equipment you use is scrupulously clean. Likewise, when handling ingredients, it's essential that your hands are really clean or wear food-handling gloves.
* Use a sterilized glass preserving jar for storing your pickles (see page 126 for our preferred method of sterilizing).
* If the pickled vegetables become slimy, mouldy or develop a visible fuzz, or have a bad or alcoholic smell, the fermentation process has been compromised and they must be thrown away. This may be due to mould or yeast contaminating the fermentation process when equipment isn't properly clean or bacteria is introduced while checking on the batch.

SAUERKRAUT

This salty and sour pickled cabbage is one of the best-known European pickles and a good place to start if you want to earn your pickling stripes (see photograph overleaf). Sauerkraut is a popular accompaniment to fried foods in the USA and makes an ideal side for our Buffalo-marinated Tofu with Crunchy Crumb Coating (see page 48).

MAKES 8–10 SERVINGS

1kg (2lb 4oz) white cabbage, halved, cored and finely sliced
500g (1lb 2oz) carrots
1 tablespoon salt
¼ teaspoon caraway seeds
2 allspice berries
1 bay leaf

1   Put the cabbage in a large bowl. Peel and finely julienne or grate the carrots, then add to the bowl with the salt. Using clean hands, firmly massage the cabbage for 5–6 minutes or longer until you are able to squeeze liquid from the cabbage. Add the remaining ingredients and mix together well.

2   Pack the mixture tightly into a still-warm sterilized 1-litre (1¾-pint) preserving jar (see page 126), pressing it down as hard as you

>>

can to eliminate most of the air bubbles. Liquid should begin to rise above the cabbage, but make sure there is at least 3cm (1¼ inches) of space between the liquid and the top of the jar, as the sauerkraut will expand as it ferments.

3 Seal the jar tightly and leave in a dry, cool place away from any direct sunlight for a minimum of 10 days to allow the cabbage to ferment, or for up to 2 or even 3 weeks if desired. Using a clean fork, taste the sauerkraut after 5–6 days to check on the development of the flavour, making sure you pack the cabbage back down until the liquid rises above it. Once you have left it to ferment long enough for your taste, transfer the jar to the refrigerator where the fermentation process will slow down considerably. Avoid checking on progress of the fermentation too often, as this may introduce bacteria, mould or yeast that will spoil the batch. If stored properly, the sauerkraut will last for months in the refrigerator.

PICKLED CUCUMBERS

**MAKES ABOUT
8–10 SERVINGS**

2 large cucumbers (about 800g/1lb 12oz total weight)

30g (1oz) dill, chopped

150g (5½oz) granulated sugar

25g (1oz) salt

500ml (18fl oz) water

250ml (9fl oz) cider vinegar

½ tablespoon wholegrain mustard

¼ teaspoon mustard powder

¼ teaspoon turmeric

A lot of pickled vegetables are heavy on the use of vinegar, and so this usually dominates the taste. But this recipe has a nice balance of sweet and tartness, allowing you to taste the cucumbers and added herbs and spices. These make a great addition to salads, burgers and sandwiches (see photograph overleaf).

1 Slice the cucumber into thin discs about 2mm (¹⁄₁₆ inch) thick. Put in a heatproof bowl with the chopped dill.

2 Heat all the remaining ingredients together in a large stainless steel saucepan over a medium heat and simmer for 4–5 minutes, giving the mixture a quick whisk with a balloon whisk to make sure all the sugar has dissolved.

3 Remove from the heat, pour the hot pickling liquid over the cucumber slices and dill and use a spoon or spatula to mix the cucumber with the liquid. Weigh the cucumber slices down with a plate, so that they are submerged in the liquid, and leave to cool.

4 Once the cucumber has cooled, transfer to 2 × 500ml (18fl oz) cooled sterilized airtight jars (see page 126) or a large plastic container along with enough pickling juice to cover them. They will keep for up to 3 weeks in the refrigerator.

SOUR DILL PICKLES

It can be hard to find pickling cucumbers, otherwise known as gherkins, but when they are in season it's best to buy in bulk and pickle as many as you can to last a few months. Pickling cucumbers are short, no more than 10–13cm (4–5 inches) in length, thick, less regularly shaped than salad cucumbers and have bumpy skin. The best place to find them would be your local farmers' market or European grocery store.

There are a couple of key ingredients to make sure your gherkins last for many months. The first is fresh oak, grape or horseradish leaves, as they contain tannins to keep the gherkins crunchy. The second is non-iodized salt, which you can buy from food stores that carry a good stock of Eastern European products as well as online, where you can also source the dried dill flowers and stems.

Having said this, we have experimented with various pickling options and have had success pickling supermarket-bought baby cucumbers with no more than some salted water and a few herbs, without the use of any of the aforementioned leaves. They were not as crunchy and probably wouldn't last sitting around for a few months, but were nonetheless very tasty.

1   Wash the gherkins under cold water and set aside. Wash and then slice the horseradish root into 4–5 slices.

2   Pack all the ingredients, except the measured water and salt, into the base of a still-warm sterilized 1-litre (1¾-pint) preserving jar (*see* page 126), then pack the gherkins into the jar as tightly as possible so that they don't float to the top when the jar is filled with water.

3   Put the measured water into a large jug, add the salt and stir until dissolved. Pour the salted water into the jar until the gherkins are covered but allowing at least 3cm (1¼ inches) of space between the liquid and the top of the jar, as the pickles will need room to ferment.

4   Seal the jar tightly and leave in a dry, cool place away from any direct sunlight for a minimum of 10 days to allow the gherkins to ferment. By that stage, they will have darkened and changed colour. You can continue to store them in a dark place for several months and open as needed.

**MAKES ABOUT
8–10 SERVINGS**

500g (1lb 2oz) fresh gherkins
   (pickling cucumbers)
5cm (2-inch) piece of fresh
   horseradish root
5 new-season green or "wet"
   garlic cloves (or regular
   garlic), peeled
4 allspice berries
1 bay leaf
1 dried dill flower and stem
   (or 2 sprigs of fresh dill)
1 large horseradish, grape
   or oak leaf
1 litre (1¾ pints) water
1 heaped tablespoon
   non-iodized salt

5   You may find it difficult to remove the lid from the jar, in which case slide a butter knife under the side of the lid to release the pressure and allow some of the air inside the jar to escape. Once the lid is off, the brine will fizz quite a lot, but this is normal and is actually a good sign that your pickles have worked. Once opened, keep the pickles refrigerated.

6   If you didn't use a horseradish, grape or oak leaf, or couldn't find gherkins and used baby cucumbers instead, the pickles may not have the best crunch to them, as mentioned in the recipe introduction, and we wouldn't recommend leaving them to ferment for more than the 10-day minimum before transferring them to the refrigerator.

BAHARAT SPICE MIX

Baharat means "spice" in Arabic and is also used in relation to allspice. In this case, it refers to our spice mix based on Lebanese seven spice, a mix that doesn't seem to have any fixed recipe; we have used a combination of eight spices, while other recipes feature only five.

As with any spice mix, the end result is much better if whole spices are used, toasted and freshly ground, but if you don't have the time or inclination, the ready-made spice mix is widely available to buy.

1   Break up the cinnamon sticks with your hands.
2   Toast the cinnamon pieces with all the other spices in a dry frying pan over a gentle heat for 2-3 minutes, stirring, until they release their aroma. Remove from the heat and then grind the spices with a pestle and mortar or an electric spice grinder.
3   Although best used fresh, the spice mix can be stored in a clean airtight jar in a cool, dry place for 4-6 weeks.

MAKES ABOUT 160G (5¾OZ)

2 cinnamon sticks
2 tablespoons black
   peppercorns
2 tablespoons coriander seeds
1 teaspoon fenugreek seeds
½ teaspoon allspice berries
1 tablespoon cumin seeds
2 teaspoons green cardamom
   pods
½ whole nutmeg, grated

BOURBON BARBECUE SAUCE

MAKES 400ML (14FL OZ)

1 tablespoon vegetable oil

½ onion, finely chopped

2 large garlic cloves, crushed

½ teaspoon chopped thyme leaves

¼ teaspoon garlic powder

¼ teaspoon ground black pepper

50ml (2fl oz) bourbon

250g (9oz) tomato ketchup

30g (1oz) chipotle chillies in adobo sauce

½ tablespoon Henderson's Relish (see page 28)

½ tablespoon soft light brown sugar

200ml (7fl oz) water

1 teaspoon tamari

1 teaspoon Dijon mustard

2 teaspoons maple syrup

grated zest and juice of ½ lime

Smoky yet sweet, this sauce is everything a barbecue glaze should be. We use this with our Memphis Bourbon Barbecue Skewers (see page 112) but it also makes a nice dip for sweet potato fries and a great condiment for vegan burgers.

1   Heat the oil in a medium-sized saucepan, add the onion with the garlic and sauté over a medium heat, stirring frequently, until translucent. Stir in the thyme, garlic powder and pepper and cook gently, stirring, for a few minutes.

2   Deglaze the pan with the bourbon and cook until slightly reduced. Mix in the remaining ingredients and bring to a simmer, then cook over a low heat for 25-30 minutes to allow the flavours to infuse into the sauce, stirring frequently so that it doesn't catch on the base of the pan.

3   Leave the sauce to cool, then blend with a stick blender.

4   Store in a clean airtight jar in the refrigerator (it will keep for up to a couple of weeks) or in the freezer.

HAZELNUT &
ALMOND DUKKAH

An Egyptian spiced nut mixture, dukkah is eaten across
the Middle East and is becoming more widely available to buy
ready prepared in the UK, but it's easy to make at home. The
taste of freshly toasted nuts and seeds is impossible to beat.
Traditionally, it's eaten by dipping warm bread into olive oil and
then into the dukkah, but you will find it a welcome addition to
a huge range of foods – roast squash, hummus, lentil soup,
grilled greens. . . the list goes on seemingly forever. So this is
a handy mixture to have around for boosting any simple meal.

1   First toast the nuts and seeds. Preheat the oven to 180°C
    (350°F), Gas Mark 4. Spread the hazelnuts and almonds out on
    a baking tray, keeping them separate. Bake for 15 minutes or so
    until the almonds have coloured a little and the hazelnut skins
    are beginning to break apart. On a separate baking tray, spread
    the sesame seeds out thinly. Bake for about 10 minutes, stirring
    occasionally to ensure they toast evenly.

2   Meanwhile, put all the whole spices in a small dry frying pan over
    a gentle heat and toast for 2–3 minutes, stirring, until they
    release their aroma. Remove from the heat and then coarsely
    grind the spices with a pestle and mortar or an electric spice
    grinder so that they still have some texture.

3   Remove the nuts and seeds from the oven. When the hazelnuts
    are cool enough to handle, tip them on to a clean tea towel,
    bunch the tea towel around the nuts to form a sack and massage
    the nuts to rub the skins off. Open the tea towel and carefully
    pick out the nuts (some will still have a little skin left on them,
    but it's fine if most of the skins have been removed).

4   Chop both the hazelnuts and almonds until broken down but
    still chunky. Mix with the ground toasted spices and toasted
    sesame seeds along with the remaining ingredients in a bowl
    until well combined.

5   Store the dukkah a clean airtight jar or container in a cool,
    dry place. It will keep for several weeks.

MAKES 10–12 SERVINGS

100g (3½oz) hazelnuts with
    their skins
100g (3½oz) whole blanched
    almonds
40g (1½oz) white sesame seeds
½ tablespoon fennel seeds
1 teaspoon cumin seeds
½ teaspoon black peppercorns
1 allspice berry
2 tablespoons coriander seeds
½ teaspoon nigella seeds
large pinch of sweet paprika
large pinch of Arbol chilli flakes
1 teaspoon sea salt flakes

DESSERTS

PASSION FRUIT & COCONUT MOUSSE CAKE

Every time we make this cake, the bakery is filled with the fragrance of passion fruit and people drifting into the kitchen to ask what the wonderful smell is. If you can buy a good-quality passion fruit purée, it will simplify making this cake no end. It's available as a cocktail ingredient and the one we use is cooked with a little sugar, though it's still very tart. But if you can't find it ready made, we've given instructions to replicate it.

1   Preheat the oven to 180°C (350°F), Gas Mark 4. Line a 23cm (9-inch) springform cake tin with baking parchment.

2   Mix the dry ingredients together in a bowl. Combine the soya milk, oil and vanilla extract or seeds in a separate large bowl, then add the dry mixture and mix together thoroughly. Pour straight into the prepared cake tin and bake for 25-30 minutes until risen and golden on top. Remove from the oven and leave to cool in the tin for a few minutes, then release from the tin and leave to cool completely on a wire rack.

3   Carefully trim off the very top layer to expose the sponge so that the coconut rum (if using) and mousse can soak in.

4   Line the cake tin again and place the cake in the base. Splash the coconut rum over the sponge if you wish.

5   Next make the mousse. If you haven't been able to find passion fruit purée, put the passion fruit pulp and seeds with the sugar and measured water in a saucepan and bring to the boil, stirring, then simmer for 10-15 minutes until the flesh has completely come away from the seeds. Remove the pan from the heat and strain the mixture through a sieve.

6   Put the passion fruit purée in a large saucepan with the coconut milk, caster sugar and agar, bring to a simmer and cook for about 10-15 minutes, whisking frequently with a balloon whisk, until all the agar has dissolved and the colour has deepened to an egg yellow. Remove from the heat, then strain through a fine-mesh sieve into a bowl and leave to cool slightly.

>>

SERVES 10-12

200g (7oz) self-raising flour
125g (4½oz) caster sugar
1 teaspoon baking powder
225ml (8fl oz) soya milk
80ml (2¾fl oz) light oil (such as groundnut or sunflower)
1 teaspoon good-quality vanilla extract or a small pinch of vanilla seeds
50ml (2fl oz) coconut rum (optional)
toasted coconut flakes, to decorate (optional)

FOR THE MOUSSE
250ml (9fl oz) passion fruit purée or 8-10 passion fruits (250ml/9fl oz pulp and seeds total quantity) with 30g (1oz) caster sugar and 100ml (3½fl oz) water
400ml (14fl oz) can full-fat coconut milk
100g (3½oz) caster sugar
8g (use gram measure for accuracy) agar agar flakes
300g (10½oz) pack silken tofu, drained
200g (7oz) pack creamed coconut, the sealed plastic pack placed in a mug of boiling water to warm and loosen the coconut

7 Blend the tofu and warmed creamed coconut together in a
blender or food processor. Then add the passion fruit mixture and
blend until smooth. Alternatively, put the tofu, warmed creamed
coconut and passion fruit mixture in a bowl and blend with a stick
blender. Pour the mixture on to the prepared sponge base and
chill in the refrigerator for 3-4 hours.

8 To make the syrup, put the passion fruit pulp and seeds, sugar
and measured water in a saucepan and bring to the boil, then
simmer for 5-10 minutes until the passion fruit seeds are
completely black and shiny and have come away from the flesh.

9 Mix the cornflour with enough water to make a smooth paste,
add to the syrup and continue to simmer for a couple of minutes,
stirring, until the mixture is glossy. Leave to cool.

10 When you are ready to serve, release the cake from the tin and
pour the syrup over the top to coat. Top with a few toasted
coconut flakes if you like.

FOR THE SYRUP
100ml (3½fl oz) passion fruit
   pulp and seeds
200g (7oz) caster sugar
250ml (9fl oz) water
½ tablespoon cornflour

AQUAFABA MERINGUES

(GF)

MAKES 6-8 MERINGUES

liquid drained from 400g
   (14oz) can good-quality
   chickpeas, which should yield
   100ml (3½fl oz) aquafaba
pinch of vanilla seeds
110g (3¾oz) caster sugar

Aquafaba is one of the most exciting vegan food discoveries of recent years. The name simply means bean water and is the starchy water that is drained from cooked pulses, but most commonly chickpeas. This liquid contains proteins from the pulses and can therefore be used in many of the ways in which egg whites are used. New applications are being discovered all the time, and one of the most exciting is that it can be whipped to high soft peaks, making vegan meringues a reality.

While aquafaba is easy to use, you can run into difficulties if it's the wrong consistency, so the basic rule of thumb is that it should be similar to that of egg whites. The liquid drained from good-quality canned or jarred chickpeas has good viscosity and should fit the bill. We've experimented with lots of different methods using cider vinegar, cornflour and so on, but have found that the plain caster sugar approach works the best.

1   Preheat the oven to 130°C (260°F), Gas Mark ¾. Line 2 large baking sheets with silicone mats or baking parchment.

2   Whisk the aquafaba in a stand mixer fitted with the whisk attachment at high speed for at least 15-20 minutes until stiff white peaks have formed.

3   Mix the vanilla seeds into the sugar. With the mixer running, add the sugar a few tablespoons at a time, whisking well after each addition until the sugar granules have dissolved before adding the next batch.

4   When all the sugar is incorporated and the meringue mixture is thick and glossy, it's ready.

5   Spoon full but not heaped large serving spoons of the meringue mixture on to the lined baking sheets, spaced apart. Alternatively, spoon the mixture into a large meringue piping bag fitted with a large piping tube.

6   Bake for 1¾-2 hours until the meringues are fairly firm on top and on the base, but check by removing one from the oven and leaving to cool for a few minutes. When ready, remove from the oven and leave to cool completely on the mats or paper. If you don't have anything else to put in the oven, you can leave them in the switched-off oven to cool.

SERVES 3-4

RHUBARB PAVLOVAS

500g (1lb 2oz) trimmed rhubarb (be choosy and trim off all the green so that you just have the lovely pink stuff), cut into 6cm (2½-inch) pieces

125g (4½oz) caster sugar

juice of 2 oranges

dash of beetroot juice, for colouring (*see* page 227; optional)

1 batch of Aquafaba Meringues mixture (*see* page 203)

1 batch of Coconut Whipped Cream (*see* page 237), to serve

We serve our vegan meringues as individual pavlovas using coconut whipping cream and fruit (*see* photograph of Rhubarb Pavlovas overleaf). We've had quite a bit of success folding fruit coulis into the meringues to get a ripple effect, and we have also used fruit powders, edible flowers or a few sesame seeds sprinkled on top before baking. However, we don't recommend folding nuts into the vegan meringue mixture, as the relatively thin consistency of the aquafaba means that the pavlovas hollow out inside as they cook. Additionally, it's important not to assemble the pavlovas until just before serving, as the meringues are more delicate than their egg cousins and the moisture from whipped cream or fruit will cause them to collapse. Here are a few suggestions for pavlovas we've successfully made.

RHUBARB PAVLOVAS

1   Preheat the oven to 190°C (375°F), Gas Mark 5. Line a baking tray with baking parchment.

2   Toss the rhubarb pieces with the sugar and orange juice in a bowl until well combined. Spread out on the lined tray to form a single layer. If the rhubarb is quite thick, bake for 10 minutes, then turn the pieces over and bake for a further 10 minutes. If the rhubarb is medium thick, reduce the cooking time to 8 minutes on each side, and if it's thin, bake for just 5 minutes per side. You will need to check how the rhubarb is doing frequently and remove from the oven just before it looks done. Leave to cool on the baking tray.

3   Drain off any syrup from the rhubarb and select 4 pieces, choosing any slightly overdone ones. Blend in a measuring jug with a stick blender to yield about 3 tablespoons of rhubarb purée. If it's not very pink, you can add a little beetroot juice to strengthen the colour.

4   Carefully fold 1-2 tablespoons of the rhubarb purée into the finished meringue mixture to achieve a ripple effect and then bake following the instructions on page 203.

5   Serve with the coconut whipped cream along with the remaining rhubarb purée and the rest of the poached rhubarb.

>>

RASPBERRY PAVLOVAS

1 To make a coulis, put the raspberries, measured water and sugar in a saucepan and bring up to a simmer. Cook gently for about 10 minutes, stirring frequently, until the raspberries have broken down and the liquid is glossy.

2 Take the pan off the heat and leave the compote to cool a little and then blend with a stick blender. Strain the mixture through a fine-mesh sieve to remove the seeds.

3 Carefully fold 1–2 tablespoons of the raspberry coulis into the finished meringue mixture to achieve a ripple effect and then bake following the instructions on page 203.

4 When you remove the meringues from the oven, sprinkle with the crushed freeze-dried raspberries. Serve with the coconut whipped cream along with the remaining raspberry coulis and the whole raspberries.

MANGO & BLACK SESAME PAVLOVAS

1 Follow the instructions on page 203 until ready to bake the meringues, then scatter over the black sesame seeds before baking.

2 Stone and peel the mango or mangoes and then dice very finely. Put one-third of the diced mango in a measuring jug with the icing sugar and lime juice and blend with a stick blender, adding enough water to make a thick coulis. Mix the blended mixture with the remaining diced mango.

3 Assemble the pavlovas with the coconut whipped cream and mango compote with a few more sesame seeds sprinkled over, together with a finishing touch of finely shredded mint leaves.

RASPBERRY PAVLOVAS

1 punnet (about 130g/4½oz) raspberries

100ml (3½fl oz) water

75g (2¾oz) caster sugar

1 batch of Aquafaba Meringues mixture (*see* page 203)

TO SERVE

about 5g (⅛oz) freeze-dried raspberries, crushed to a dust

1 batch of Coconut Whipped Cream (*see* page 237)

1 punnet (about 130g/4½oz) raspberries

MANGO AND BLACK SESAME PAVLOVAS

1 batch of Aquafaba Meringues mixture (*see* page 203)

2 tablespoons black sesame seeds, plus extra for sprinkling on top

1 large or 2 small ripe mangoes (we prefer to use honey mangoes here, in which case you need 2)

2 tablespoons icing sugar

juice of 1 lime

TO SERVE

1 batch of Coconut Whipped Cream (*see* page 237)

mint leaves, finely shredded

PEACH MELBA
WITH RASPBERRY COMPOTE & LEMON SHORTBREAD SHARDS

SERVES 4-6

4–6 perfectly ripe peaches
150ml (5fl oz) water
rind of 1 lemon, cut into thin
  strips, and the juice
80g (3oz) caster sugar
pinch of vanilla seeds

**FOR THE LEMON
  SHORTBREAD**

125g (4½oz) plain flour,
  plus extra for dusting
15g (½oz) cornflour
50g (1¾oz) caster sugar,
  plus extra for topping
1 teaspoon sea salt flakes
grated zest of 1 lemon
100g (3½oz) Coconut Butter
  (*see* page 247), chilled

TO SERVE

vegan vanilla ice cream
1 batch of Berry Compote,
  either version, made with
  raspberries (*see* page 18)
75ml (5 tablespoons) peach
  schnapps (optional)

The esteemed French chef Auguste Escoffier claimed to have invented the Peach Melba in the early 1890s at the Savoy Hotel in London, in honour of the Australian soprano Nellie Melba, who was a guest at the hotel while performing at Covent Garden. Conjuring up images of *Abigail's Party*, it's as cute and kitsch as it is refreshingly yummy.

The method we use to poach peaches in the oven is very simple, and if you want to cut down on prep you can just serve them with fresh raspberries, though the compote is both lovely and traditional. We make the shortbread using our special homemade vegan Coconut Butter (*see* page 247), but it can be made with vegan margarine instead, which will result in a slightly softer biscuit.

1. Preheat the oven to 200°C (400°F), Gas Mark 6. Cut each peach in half along the seam, twist the 2 halves in opposite directions to separate and remove the stone. Place the peaches, cut side down, in an ovenproof dish, cover with the measured water and add the lemon rind and juice, sugar and vanilla seeds. Bake for 15–20 minutes (the exact timing will depend on how ripe the peaches are) until the skins are beginning to wrinkle.

2. Remove from the oven, then transfer the peaches to a bowl, cover with clingfilm and leave to cool. Once cooled, you should be able to remove the skins easily. Drain the peach halves from the bowl of syrup, reserving any juices that escape when cutting, then return to the bowl of syrup with any of the reserved juices.

3. To make the shortbread, preheat the oven to 240°C (475°F), Gas Mark 9.

4. Measure all the dry ingredients into a bowl, add the lemon zest and mix together. Grate in the coconut butter using the large-holed side of a box grater. Pinch the butter into the flour mixture with your fingertips to achieve a fine crumb. Then gently knead the mixture together to form a ball of dough.

>>

5   Cut a piece of baking parchment large enough to cover your baking sheet, or use a silicone mat. Lightly flour the parchment or mat and roll out the shortbread dough into a disc about 30cm (12 inches) in diameter and 5mm (¼ inch) thick.

6   Carefully lift the baking parchment or silicone mat and shortbread dough on to the baking sheet. Scatter the dough with caster sugar and score the surface with lines like a clock face into 8–10 equal pieces. Place in the oven and immediately reduce the oven temperature to 180°C (350°F), Gas Mark 4. Bake for 15 minutes until the shortbread is crisp and golden.

7   When cool, snap the shortbread into shards along the scored lines.

8   To assemble, give each person 3 or 4 pieces of peach with some of the peachy syrup on a plate, add a scoop or two of your favourite vegan vanilla ice cream and drizzle the raspberry compote on top. Serve with lemon shortbread shards. If you wish, you can add a tot of peach schnapps on top.

RASPBERRY, ALMOND, SHERRY & SAFFRON TRIFLE

There is nothing quite like a trifle to round off a special meal with all its glistening layers of sponge, creamy custard, bright fruit compote, cream and toasted nuts. The raspberries make it a summery dessert, but you can use any seasonal fruit you like – we've made a lovely spiced cranberry version and one with poached peaches. To cut down on labour on the day, you can make the sponge and raspberry compote in advance. If you prefer, you can forgo the compote and just use a layer of fresh berries, though it does create a real depth of flavour.

1   Preheat the oven to 180°C (350°F), Gas Mark 4. Line a 23cm (9-inch) round cake tin with baking parchment.

2   Put all the dry ingredients into a large bowl and mix together with a small balloon whisk. Measure out the wet ingredients into a jug and again mix together with the whisk. Pour the wet ingredients into the dry mixture and mix until well combined, then pour into the lined cake tin. Bake for 30 minutes until well risen and the sponge springs back to the touch.

3   Remove from the oven and leave to cool for a few minutes in the tin, then turn out on to a wire rack and leave to cool completely.

4   To make the custard, put all the ingredients, except the cornflour, in a pan and heat gently, stirring frequently, until warm. Mix the cornflour with enough cold water to make a smooth paste. Add to the almond-milk mixture and cook for a few minutes, stirring, until thickened. Remove the pan from the heat. You can strain the custard through a sieve to remove any lumps. Leave to cool.

5   To assemble, cut the sponge into slices 2.5cm (1 inch) thick and use to line the base of a glass trifle dish, 20cm (8 inches) in diameter with a flat base, evenly. Pour the sherry evenly over the sponge, then spoon over an even layer of raspberry compote. Leave in the refrigerator for 20 minutes or so to settle before carefully spooning over the custard. Cover and leave the custard to set in the refrigerator for a few hours.

6   Before serving, pipe the freshly whipped coconut cream on top of the trifle. Alternatively, add in small spoonfuls and spread out evenly across the top, then heat the spoon in hot water and use it to smooth the surface of the cream. Finally, scatter with the toasted almonds and decorate with the raspberries if you like.

SERVES 6–8

200g (7oz) self-raising flour
160g (5¾oz) caster sugar
60g (2¼oz) ground almonds
1½ teaspoons baking powder
250ml (9fl oz) soya milk
100ml (3½fl oz) light oil (such as groundnut or sunflower)
1 teaspoon good-quality vanilla extract

FOR THE CUSTARD

1.5 litres (2¾ pints) almond milk
180g (6¼oz) caster sugar
2 teaspoons good-quality vanilla extract
pinch of vanilla seeds
pinch of saffron threads (about 10)
80g (3oz) cornflour

TO ASSEMBLE

125ml (4fl oz) Pedro Ximénez sherry
1 batch of Berry Compote, cooked version, made with raspberries, (see page 18), cooled
2 batches of Coconut Whipped Cream (see page 237)
50g (1¾oz) toasted flaked almonds
10 raspberries (optional)

BRAMLEY APPLE, BLACKBERRY & OAT CRUMBLE

We change the fruit for our crumble every couple of days at Mildreds, but the classic combination of apple and blackberry remains a firm favourite. Wild blackberries are to be found in most areas of the UK and Europe, as well as Eastern and coastal West USA, so can be easily foraged – just remember to wear long sleeves and gloves! If you prefer, you can switch out the blackberries for raspberries, strawberries or blueberries, while keeping the quantity of apples as specified.

   This is one recipe where our homemade vegan butter has been a real game changer, but if you're pressed for time you can use vegan margarine.

1   For the crumble top, preheat the oven to 170°C (340°F), Gas Mark 3½. Line a baking sheet with baking parchment.
2   Measure out the crumble ingredients into a large bowl and mix together. Transfer, in batches, to a food processor and pulse to a crumb consistency, returning to the bowl. Then mix together again.
3   Spread the crumble mix out on the lined baking sheet and bake for 20–25 minutes, stirring occasionally. Remove from the oven and leave to cool on the sheet.
4   Increase the oven temperature to 220°C (425°F), Gas Mark 7.
5   Toss the prepared apples in the sugar and flour in a bowl, then turn out into a baking dish or a lined roasting tray and bake for 15–20 minutes until holding their shape but soft to the touch. Stir in the blackberries and vanilla seeds and bake for a further 5–10 minutes. Check the sweetness at this point – fruit does vary quite a lot in this regard, so you may need to add a bit more sugar. Equally, the apples and berries may release more liquid sometimes, so if the mixture looks a bit wet, strain off any excess.
6   Transfer the fruit mixture to your ovenproof crumble dish – we use a 25cm (10-inch) oval Pyrex dish. The fruit layer should be about 4cm (1½ inches) deep. Top with the crumble top and bake for 15–20 minutes until the top of the crumble is beginning to brown.
7   Serve the crumble warm with the vegan cream, vegan crème Anglaise or vegan ice cream.

SERVES 6-8

6 large Bramley apples, peeled, cored and cut into 3cm (1¼-inch) cubes
200g (7oz) caster sugar, or more to taste
1 tablespoon plain flour
150g (5½oz) fresh or frozen blackberries
pinch of vanilla seeds
vegan single cream, Vegan Crème Anglaise (*see* page 238) or vegan ice cream, to serve

FOR THE CRUMBLE TOP
250g (9oz) plain flour
100g (3½oz) jumbo rolled oats
150g (5½oz) demerara sugar
200g (7oz) Coconut Butter (*see* page 247), chilled
2 teaspoons ground cinnamon
1 tablespoon sea salt flakes

ESPRESSO CRÈME CARAMEL
WITH PISTACHIO BISCOTTI

**MAKES 6 CRÈME
CARAMELS AND
10-15 BISCOTTI**

200g (7oz) caster sugar
about 75ml (5 tablespoons)
   water

FOR THE ESPRESSO CRÈME
2 × 400ml (14oz) cans full-fat
   coconut milk (we use the
   Aroy-D brand for this)
about 50ml (2fl oz) freshly
   brewed espresso (quantity is
   approximate because we
   don't know how strong your
   espresso is!)
100g (3½oz) caster sugar
3g (use gram measure for
   accuracy) agar agar flakes
tiny pinch of vanilla seeds

This is a proper grown-up dessert and ideal for a dinner party or special occasion meal, as it can be prepared in advance. In fact, the crème caramel is very much the better for being allowed to sit for 12 hours or more. You might think that since the main ingredient here is coconut milk it would have a coconut flavour, but we have found that the coffee and caramel neutralize it.

Some people are intimidated by the concept of caramel, but it's very simple to make if you don't fiddle around with it too much. Never stir or whisk caramel as it cooks or the sugar will crystallize around the edge of the pan and you'll end up with a lumpy mess. Also, you must work fast once the caramelization occurs, as the sugar will continue to cook otherwise. The sugar is very hot once caramelized, so it's best not to have kids around while you're making it, and don't be tempted to stick your finger in it to taste.

The biscotti are a little extra effort, but they are a simple biscuit to make and keep for ages. We have two Italian lads (non-vegan) working in the bakery and they love these - enough said!

1   Place 6 metal dariole moulds or ramekins on a heatproof mat or chopping board ready to use.

2   Put the sugar in a saucepan and add the measured water - just enough to make all the sugar wet. Bring to the boil, without stirring, and simmer until the sugar starts to catch, that is when dark caramel spots begin to appear. (This takes 5-10 minutes, but don't be tempted to leave the room because you might come back to a pan full of smoking black tar.) Once the sugar has reached this stage, give the pan a quick swirl and then continue to cook until it reaches an even orange brown (caramel) colour.

3   Quickly coat the base of each dariole mould or ramekin with about 2 tablespoons of the caramel. This is where you need to work fast, as the caramel will continue cooking.

4   Next make the espresso crème. Place all the ingredients into a saucepan, adding just enough espresso to achieve a café latte colour and flavour, and bring to a simmer. Simmer gently for about 10-15 minutes, whisking frequently with a balloon whisk, until all the agar has dissolved. Remove from the heat and strain through a fine-mesh sieve.

5   Pour the espresso crème into the moulds and refrigerate for 12-24 hours until ready to serve.

>>

FOR THE PISTACHIO BISCOTTI

2 tablespoons cornflour

2½ tablespoons orange juice

200g (7oz) plain flour

1 teaspoon baking powder

¼ teaspoon salt

80g (3oz) roasted, unsalted shelled pistachio nuts, roughly ground

grated zest of ½ orange

100g (3½oz) caster sugar

60ml (4 tablespoons) almond milk

1 tablespoon melted coconut oil

1 teaspoon good-quality vanilla extract

vegan single cream, for brushing

demerara sugar, for sprinkling

75g (2¾oz) vegan dark chocolate (minimum 70% cocoa solids), melted (*see* page 230), to decorate (optional)

6 To make the biscotti, preheat the oven to 190°C (375°F), Gas Mark 5. Line a large baking sheet with baking parchment.

7 Mix the cornflour with the orange juice to make a smooth paste and set aside.

8 Measure out the flour, baking powder, salt and ground pistachios into a bowl, add the orange zest and mix together.

9 Beat the sugar with the almond milk, melted coconut oil and vanilla extract in a stand mixer fitted with the paddle attachment, or with a hand-held electric mixer in a bowl, until frothy. Add the cornflour paste and whisk for a further 3 minutes or so. Fold in the flour mixture until a dough forms.

10 Divide the dough into 2 flattened loaves about 7.5cm (3 inches) wide and about 2.5cm (1 inch) thick. Transfer to the lined baking tray, then brush with a little vegan cream and sprinkle with demerara sugar. Bake for 35 minutes.

11 Remove from the oven and leave to cool for about 10 minutes.

12 Using a sharp bread or serrated knife, cut each loaf on a slight diagonal into slices about 1cm (½ inch) thick. (Don't worry if you lose a few in the cutting process.) Lay the slices carefully on the lined baking sheet and bake for a further 20 minutes, flipping over halfway through.

13 Remove from the oven and leave to cool, then drizzle with the melted chocolate, if you like.

14 To turn the crème caramels out, hold each mould with your hand over the top and give the caramel a small firm shake from side to side. It should loosen inside the mould. Place a plate on top and turn both the mould and plate over together. The crème caramel should come away when you lift the mould. Serve with the biscotti.

BLACK TEA, STOUT & SPICED RUM CHRISTMAS PUDDING

The steaming may seem like a faff, but the great thing about Christmas pudding is that you can make it far in advance of the big day, so it's one less job to do in the immediate run-up to the festivities. This is a totally versatile recipe in which you can change the dried fruit to any you prefer, add nuts and omit or change the booze, just as long as you keep the quantities of fruit and liquid the same; for example, if you decide to leave out the alcohol, then add more tea.

Feel free to skip the feeding stage if you wish, which is for those of you who like quite a boozy pudding to send you quietly to sleep after your lunch.

1   Measure out the dried fruit, marmalade, flour, sugar, spices, breadcrumbs and suet into a large bowl and mix together. Measure out the milk and treacle or syrup into a jug and stir to combine, then mix in the stout, spiced rum and tea. Pour the wet mixture into the dry mixture and stir to combine, then fold in the grated apple and orange zest.

2   Grease a 1-litre (1¾-pint) pudding bowl with vegan margarine and scrape all the pudding mixture into it. Cover the top with a round of baking parchment. If the pudding bowl has a lid, grease it and then attach it. Otherwise, cover the top with a double thickness of muslin tied around the lip of the bowl with kitchen string. Cover the whole bowl in clingfilm and then in foil to ensure it is completely sealed.

3   Place a heatproof saucer or small plate in the base of a large saucepan and place the pudding on top. Add enough water to come up about halfway up the side of pudding bowl. Cover the saucepan and bring to the boil, then reduce the heat and steam the pudding for 4 hours, checking the water level occasionally and topping up when necessary.

4   Remove the pudding from the heat and leave to cool completely, then store in the refrigerator for up to 4 weeks.

>>

MAKES 1 × 1-LITRE (1¾-PINT) PUDDING; SERVES 6-8

100g (3½oz) sultanas
100g (3½oz) currants
100g (3½oz) chopped pitted prunes
20g (¾oz) glacé cherries, halved
30g (1oz) candied peel
(or any mixture of dried fruit or dried fruit and nuts – traditionally chopped blanched almonds – of your choice totalling 350g/12oz)
40g (1½oz) chunky marmalade
75g (2¾oz) self-raising flour
100g (3½oz) soft dark brown sugar (preferably) or soft light brown sugar
1 teaspoon ground cinnamon
½ teaspoon grated nutmeg
80g (3oz) fresh white breadcrumbs
60g (2½oz) vegetarian suet
50ml (2fl oz) plant-based milk
1 tablespoon black treacle or maple or golden syrup
50ml (2fl oz) stout
50ml (2fl oz) spiced rum
2 tablespoons strongly brewed black tea
150g (5½oz) grated dessert apple (about 1 large)
grated zest of 1 orange
vegan margarine, for greasing

Vegan Crème Anglaise (*see page 238*), vegan single cream or vegan ice cream

TO FEED

75ml (5 tablespoons) spiced rum, plus extra to serve (optional)

2 tablespoons strongly brewed black tea

5   About 2 weeks or so before you are due to serve the pudding, start the feeding process. Mix the spiced rum and tea together in a jug. Unwrap the pudding and pierce the top in 3 or 4 places with a clean metal or wooden skewer, then sprinkle a little of the rum mixture over the top, repeating every day or every 2 days.

6   To prepare the Christmas pudding to serve, rewrap and steam the pudding as before but for 1-1½ hours. Alternatively, to reheat in an 800W microwave oven, loosen the lid of the pudding bowl or wrap the bowl in clingfilm and pierce a couple of holes in the top (don't use foil). Microwave on full power for 4 minutes and then leave to stand for 3 minutes. Next, microwave on low/ defrost for 4 minutes and then leave to stand for 5 minutes.

7   Turn the pudding out on to a plate and then, if you wish, heat a little spiced rum in a saucepan, turn off the lights and set it on fire, then pour the rum over the pudding and carry to the table, obviously removing any trip hazards (such as small children) before doing so!

8   Serve the pudding warm with crème Anglaise, vegan single cream or vegan ice cream – or all 3 (we're not judging you).

RAW CHOCOLATE MOUSSE CAKE
WITH DATE & ALMOND CRUST

A really popular summer menu addition of recent years, this raw cake is really easy to make and uses no refined sugar. We were so shocked the first time we made this, having assumed that all these nutritious ingredients like dates and avocado would result in a worthy-tasting cake. How wrong we were! The smooth truffle-like filling is mega rich, so you won't need a big slice.

If you're pressed for time, you can forgo the crust and just make the filling, as it will set firmly enough to cut. We sometimes fold fresh berries into the mixture.

1 Firstly, line the sides of a 23cm (9-inch) springform cake tin with baking parchment.

2 Add all the ingredients to a food processor, or use a stick blender fitted with the chopping/drum attachment, and pulse until you have a chunky paste.

3 Press the crust paste into the base and about 3cm (1¼ inches) up the side of the prepared cake tin.

4 For the mousse filling, put all the ingredients in the food processor or a blender and blend together until completely smooth, making sure there are no lumps of avocado remaining. Scoop the mixture on to the crust base and then smooth over.

5 Chill in the refrigerator preferably overnight or for at least 6 hours. We find that if you eat it the same day, you do get a slight avocado flavour, which disappears when it has time to sit.

6 Decorate the top with the coarsely ground cocoa nibs. We've also used berries or lavender or other fresh edible flowers to nice effect.

MAKES 1 × 23CM (9-INCH) CAKE; SERVES 8-10

170g (6oz) flaked almonds
170g (6oz) pitted dried dates
25g (1oz) raw cocoa powder
½ teaspoon sea salt flakes
2 tablespoons agave syrup
30g (1oz) coarsely ground raw cocoa nibs, to decorate
mixed berries or fresh edible flowers, to serve (optional)

FOR THE MOUSSE FILLING
2 ripe Hass avocados, stoned, peeled and roughly chopped
150g (5½oz) raw coconut sugar
80g (3oz) raw cocoa powder
60g (2¼oz) coconut oil
pinch of vanilla powder
230ml (8fl oz) almond milk
130g (4¾oz) coconut cream

DARK CHOCOLATE BLACK CHERRY FONDANT

There's something about cutting into a pudding and finding it full of hot chocolate that gives you a child-like ripple of joy. These warm, rich, fudgy, truffle-centred little puddings are not hard to make and microwave beautifully to reheat, so can be made in advance. But if you're planning on reheating them, err on the side of caution when it comes to how long you bake them, making sure they are just cooked and not too firm.

The pudding mixture will also work with firm tofu, but silken tofu has a slightly better texture. You could place any vegan truffle in the centre of these if you don't have time to make truffles from scratch.

1   Preheat the oven to 170°C (340°F), Gas Mark 3½. Oil 6 cups of a nonstick muffin tray.

2   Put all the dry ingredients in a bowl, or in the bowl of a stand mixer fitted with the whisk attachment, and mix thoroughly.

3   Blend the remaining ingredients, except the truffles, in a blender, or in a measuring jug with a stick blender, until smooth.

4   Add the wet mixture to the bowl, or mixer bowl, containing the dry mixture. Whisk together using a stick blender fitted with the whisk attachment or a hand-held electric whisk or with the mixer until smooth and fully incorporated. Don't leave the mixture to stand for too long because the raising agents have been activated, so use immediately.

5   Spoon about 2cm (¾ inch) of the fondant mixture into each muffin cup and then place a truffle in the centre. Cover the truffle with another 1.5-2cm (⅝-¾ inch) of fondant mixture, then bang the tray down on the work surface to settle so that the cups are almost full but with a space of about 5mm (¼ inch) left at the top.

6   Bake for 12-14 minutes until risen and fairly firm to the touch.

7   Serve warm with vegan ice cream or vegan single cream.

MAKES 6 FONDANTS

75g (2¾oz) gluten-free
   plain flour
60g (2¼oz) light muscovado
   sugar
25g (1oz) vegan cocoa powder
½ tsp gluten-free baking
   powder
pinch of ground cinnamon
pinch of salt
70g (2½oz) silken tofu
75ml (5 tablespoons) soya milk
grated zest of ½ orange
1 tablespoon vegetable oil,
   plus extra for oiling
1 tablespoon maple syrup
¼ teaspoon good-quality
   vanilla extract
6 Maraschino Cherry Truffles
   (*see* page 225) or other vegan
   truffles
vegan ice cream or vegan
   single cream, to serve

DARK CHOCOLATE TRUFFLES

MAKES 12-14 TRUFFLES

DARK CHOCOLATE
   TRUFFLES

40g (1½oz) soya cream

85g (3oz) vegan dark
   chocolate (minimum 70%
   cocoa solids), broken into
   small pieces

85g (3oz) vegan cocoa powder,
   for coating

light oil (such as groundnut or
   sunflower), for oiling
   (optional)

TURKISH ROSE AND
   PISTACHIO TRUFFLES

100g (3½oz) raw shelled
   pistachio nuts

1 tablespoon dried rose petals

1 batch of Dark Chocolate
   Truffle mixture (*see* above)

⅛ teaspoon good-quality
   rosewater, or to taste

Wayne Glass, one of our very talented pastry chefs, introduced vegan truffles to our dessert menus and we've featured a different flavour every menu change since. They are a lovely way to round off a special meal and also make a great gift. The truffle base couldn't be simpler to make and then you can play around with adding different ingredients such as nuts, alcohol and fruits. The plain truffle is very good in itself but we've given you four of Wayne's most popular variants as well. The truffles will keep for 3-4 weeks in an airtight container in the refrigerator if they don't contain any fresh additional ingredients.

DARK CHOCOLATE TRUFFLES

1   Heat the soya cream in a small saucepan until almost boiling, then remove from the heat, add the chocolate and whisk with a balloon whisk until fully combined.

2   Transfer to a small bowl or container and leave to cool completely.

3   Once the truffle mixture has cooled, pour boiling water into a cup. Put the cocoa in a bowl and set out an airtight container for the finished truffles. Dip a melon baller or small spoon into the hot water to heat up and tap off any excess water, then scoop a ball of the truffle mixture about the size of a cherry. Roll in your hands to make it evenly round and drop into the cocoa to coat, then transfer to the container. It's best to work in batches, scooping out about 5 balls of truffle mixture at a time, to minimize mess. (You can work a small amount of oil into your hands before starting to shape the truffles to stop the mixture sticking to them too much.)

TURKISH ROSE & PISTACHIO TRUFFLES

1   Preheat the oven to 180°C (350°F), Gas Mark 4. Line a baking sheet with baking parchment.

2   Spread the pistachios out on the lined baking sheet and toast for 10-15 minutes until fragrant and slightly coloured. Remove from the oven and leave to cool.

3   Put the nuts in a food processor with the dried rose petals, or use a stick blender fitted with the chopping/drum attachment, and pulse until coarsely ground together - go carefully, as you don't want to overgrind accidently and make nut butter! Alternatively, chop the nuts and dried rose petals very finely by hand.

>>

TOASTED COCONUT AND RUM TRUFFLES

100g (3½oz) desiccated coconut, for coating

1 batch of Dark Chocolate Truffle mixture (*see* page 223)

2 tablespoons coconut rum

AMARETTO AND ALMOND TRUFFLES

100g (3½oz) flaked almonds, for coating

1 batch of Dark Chocolate Truffle mixture (*see* page 223)

2 tablespoons Amaretto

MARASCHINO CHERRY TRUFFLES

1 batch of Dark Chocolate Truffle mixture (*see* page 223)

2 tablespoons cherry brandy

400g (14oz) jar Maraschino cherries, drained

85g (3oz) vegan cocoa powder, for coating

---

4   Follow the instructions on page 223 to make the truffle mixture, adding the rosewater and 20g (¾oz) of the rose and pistachio mixture just after you have whisked in the chocolate while the truffle mixture is still hot.

5   Follow the instructions for shaping the truffles, but use the remaining rose and pistachio mixture for coating instead of cocoa.

TOASTED COCONUT & RUM TRUFFLES

1   Preheat the oven to 180°C (350°F), Gas Mark 4. Line a baking sheet with baking parchment.

2   Spread the desiccated coconut out on the lined baking sheet and toast for 4–5 minutes until fragrant and slightly coloured. Check on the coconut frequently, as it can turn from white to burned all too quickly. Remove from the oven and leave to cool.

3   Follow the instructions on page 223 to make the truffle mixture, adding the coconut rum just after you have whisked in the chocolate while the truffle mixture is still hot.

4   Follow the instructions for shaping the truffles, but use the toasted coconut for coating instead of cocoa.

AMARETTO & ALMOND TRUFFLES

1   Preheat the oven to 180°C (350°F), Gas Mark 4. Line a baking sheet with baking parchment. Spread the flaked almonds out on the lined baking sheet and toast for 10–15 minutes until fragrant and slightly coloured. Remove from the oven and leave to cool.

2   Put the nuts in a food processor, or use a stick blender fitted with the chopping/drum attachment, and pulse until coarsely ground - proceed with caution, as you don't want to overgrind accidently and make nut butter! Alternatively, chop the nuts very finely by hand.

3   Follow the instructions on page 223 to make the truffle mixture, adding the Amaretto just after you have whisked in the chocolate while the truffle mixture is still hot.

4   Follow the instructions for shaping the truffles, but use the toasted almonds for coating instead of cocoa.

MARASCHINO CHERRY TRUFFLES

1   Follow the instructions on page 223 to make the truffle mixture, adding the cherry brandy just after you have whisked in the chocolate while the truffle mixture is still hot.

2   Follow the instructions for shaping the truffles into balls, but then insert your thumb into each ball and add a Maraschino cherry to the centre.

3   Close the truffle mixture around the cherry and reshape into a ball before rolling in the cocoa to coat.

LITTLE PARTY CAKES

A colourful spread complete with fancy little fairy and butterfly cakes is everyone's idea of a good children's party. But our better understanding and recognition of food intolerances and allergies has meant that many parents now regard these occasions as a minefield and their children struggle to enjoy such traditional party fare. These easy vegan cakes (*see* photographs overleaf) can all be successfully made with gluten-free flour and baking powder in place of the regular wheat flour and baking powder if required. That way, no one has to miss out on the best bit of the party!

FAIRY SPONGE CAKES

1   Preheat the oven to 190°C (375°F), Gas Mark 5. Line a 12-cup fairy cake tray with fairy cake cases.

2   If you have one, prepare a piping bag by standing it open in a measuring jug. This will enable you to pipe the cake mixture quickly and neatly into the cases. Otherwise, just use 2 tablespoons.

3   Sift the dry ingredients into a bowl and mix together. Measure out all the wet ingredients into a jug and mix together. Add the wet mixture to the dry mixture and stir together with a spoon until well combined.

4   Scrape the cake mixture into the piping bag and pipe about a heaped tablespoon into each case, or use the 2 tablespoons, one to scoop and one to scrape, filling them about 8mm ($^3/_8$ inch) from the top of the case.

5   Bake for 15-20 minutes until risen and golden on top. Leave to cool in the tray for a few minutes, then transfer to a wire rack to cool completely before icing.

BUTTERCREAM ICING

1   Put the margarine and vanilla in the bowl of a stand mixer fitted with the paddle attachment and cream on a medium speed for 5 minutes. Alternatively, beat by hand with a wooden spoon in a large bowl.

2   With the mixer still running, pour in the coconut oil until incorporated, or, if making by hand, pour into the bowl in a slow, steady stream while beating constantly.

3   Add the icing sugar and cream for about 5-8 minutes in the mixer, or by hand with the spoon, until fluffy.

>>

MAKES 10-12 CAKES

FAIRY SPONGE CAKES
200g (7oz) self-raising flour
125g (4½oz) caster sugar
1 teaspoon baking powder
200ml (7fl oz) soya milk
  (or other plant-based milk)
100ml (3½fl oz) light oil
  (such as sunflower)
1 teaspoon good-quality
  vanilla extract

FOR THE BUTTERCREAM ICING
100g (3½oz) vegan margarine
½ teaspoon good-quality
  vanilla extract
2 tablespoons melted coconut oil
400g (14oz) icing sugar, sifted

BUTTERFLY CAKES

1 batch of Fairy Sponge Cakes
   (*see* opposite)

1 batch of Buttercream Icing
   (*see* opposite)

sprinkles, glacé cherries or
   other items of your choice,
   to decorate

CHOCOLATE FAIRY OR
BUTTERFLY CAKES

1 batch of Fairy Sponge Cake
   mixture (*see* opposite) but
   reducing the quantity of
   self-raising flour to 160g
   (5¾oz) and adding 30g (1oz)
   of sifted vegan cocoa powder

20g (¾oz) sifted vegan
   cocoa powder, for the icing

PINK FAIRY CAKES

1 batch of Fairy Sponge Cake
   mixture (*see* opposite) but
   using 125ml (4fl oz) soya milk
   and 75ml (5 tablespoons)
   beetroot juice

glacé cherries or other items of
   choice, to decorate

FOR THE ICING

200g (7oz) icing sugar

1 teaspoon beetroot juice

1 teaspoon orange juice

1 teaspoon vegan single cream
   (or plant-based milk)

BUTTERFLY CAKES

1   Cook a batch of Fairy Sponge Cakes following the instructions opposite. Allow the cakes to cool.

2   Using a sharp knife, gently cut a disc from the top of each cooled cake that is deeper in the centre and set aside.

3   Put the buttercream in a piping bag and pipe a heaped tablespoon of buttercream into the hollow of each cake.

4   Cut each sponge disc in half and then press into the buttercream on either side of the cake to resemble the wings of a butterfly.

5   Decorate the cakes as desired.

CHOCOLATE FAIRY OR BUTTERFLY CAKES

1   Follow the instructions for making the cakes opposite but reduce the quantity of self-raising flour to 160g (5¾oz) and add 30g (1oz) of sifted vegan cocoa powder.

2   Follow the instructions for making the buttercream icing opposite, but add 20g (¾oz) sifted vegan cocoa powder with the icing sugar.

PINK FAIRY CAKES

They don't have to be pink, obviously, but we just love the colour that the beetroot juice gives these little cakes instead of using artificial food colouring. If you don't have a juicer, finely grate a peeled raw beetroot, put in a sieve and squeeze the juice out by pressing the beetroot with the back of a spoon.

1   Follow the instructions for making the cake mixture opposite, but mix the beetroot juice with the reduced quantity of soya milk and the other wet ingredients, then bake as instructed.

2   For the icing, sift the icing sugar into a small bowl, add the remaining ingredients and whisk together with a small balloon whisk or hand-held electric whisk, carefully at first and then with vigour. If it's a little too thick, add 1-2 teaspoons extra of any of the liquid ingredients but only very gradually, as you can easily add too much.

3   Add a teaspoon of the icing to each cake and then decorate as you wish - a glacé cherry is a perennial favourite.

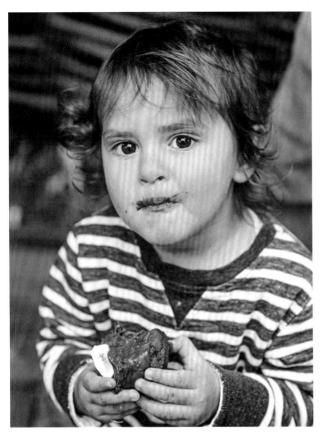

CHOCOLATE BANANA CUPCAKES
WITH CHOCOLATE FUDGE ICING

This is one of those great recipes that will have people refusing to believe it doesn't contain dairy. The bananas provide the binding quality of egg and the moisture of butter, without the fat. And while the cakes aren't good for you exactly, they are better for you than standard chocolate cake without compromising on taste. Because of the fruit, they will stay moist for longer too.

1 Preheat the oven to 190°C (375°F), Gas Mark 5. Line 12-15 cups of a muffin tray or trays with muffin cases.

2 If you have one, prepare a piping bag by standing it open in a measuring jug. This will enable you to pipe the cake mixture quickly and neatly into the cases. Otherwise, just use 2 tablespoons.

3 Put the sugar, oil and agave or maple syrup in the bowl of a stand mixer fitted with the paddle attachment and beat for a few minutes until well combined and the sugar is beginning to dissolve. Alternatively, beat by hand with a wooden spoon in a large bowl.

4 Add the banana and vanilla extract and beat again for a few minutes until well combined.

5 Measure out all the dry ingredients into a bowl and mix together with a balloon whisk, then fold into the cake mixture until well combined.

6 Quickly scrape the cake mixture into the piping bag and pipe it into the cases, or use the 2 tablespoons, one to scoop and one to scrape, filling them about 5mm (¼ inch) from the top of the case.

7 Bake for 20-25 minutes until they are risen and the sponge springs back to the touch. Leave to cool in the tray(s) for a few minutes, then transfer to a wire rack to cool completely before icing.

8 To make the fudge icing, sift the icing sugar and cocoa into the bowl of a stand mixer fitted with the paddle attachment, or into a bowl if making by hand.

9 Melt the chocolate in a heatproof bowl set over a saucepan of barely simmering water or in a microwave-proof bowl in the microwave in short bursts, stirring frequently. Add the vegan cream, golden syrup and orange zest and juice, if using, and mix together.

10 Add the chocolate mix to the dry mix and beat with the mixer or with a wooden spoon until smooth. Leave the icing to cool slightly. Then scoop a heaped tablespoon on to each of the cupcakes. Decorate with a few cocoa nibs or banana chips if you like.

MAKES 12-15 CUPCAKES

160g (5¾oz) soft light brown sugar

80g (3oz) coconut oil, melted (or any light oil such as sunflower or groundnut)

3 tablespoons agave or maple syrup

400g (14oz) peeled and mashed ripe bananas

1 teaspoon good-quality vanilla extract

220g (8oz) self-raising flour

40g (1½oz) vegan cocoa powder

2½ teaspoons baking powder

1 teaspoon ground cinnamon

100g (3½oz) vegan dark chocolate chips (minimum 70% cocoa solids)

raw cocoa nibs or banana chips, to decorate (optional)

FOR THE FUDGE ICING

250g (9oz) icing sugar

30g (1oz) vegan cocoa powder

100g (3½oz) vegan dark chocolate chips or dark chocolate bar (minimum 70% cocoa solids), broken into pieces

100ml (3½fl oz) vegan single cream

1 tablespoon golden syrup

grated zest and juice of 1 orange (optional)

FUZZY GREEN FIG BALLS

MAKES 12-15 BALLS

8 good-quality dried figs
(or dried apricots or pitted
dried dates), soaked in cold
water for 12 hours or, if you
aren't a raw purist, soaked
in hot water in an airtight
container for 30 minutes

110g (3¾oz) flaked almonds

70g (2½oz) raw shelled
pistachio nuts

100g (3½oz) desiccated
coconut, plus extra for
coating

2 tablespoons chia seeds

1 teaspoon spirulina

4 tablespoons agave syrup
(or maple syrup or raw
coconut nectar)

about 4 tablespoons water

Our fun green take on what have become known as energy balls, protein balls or power balls, these mini green spheres are super cute and provide a perfect little energy kick, as well as being raw and containing no refined sugar. They have loads of healthy fibre and nutrition from the fruit, nuts and spirulina, and are surprisingly fragrant and yummy. You can swap a lot of the ingredients here as long as you stick to roughly the same proportions, making them perfect for fussy kids. You can replace the spirulina with the same quantity of vegan cocoa powder to make a chocolate version. The nuts can be varied, although if you use a more fibrous nut like walnut, you may need more water, and if you use peanut butter or tahini, slightly less.

1 Drain the figs, then remove the tough stems.
2 Pulse the nuts in a food processor to break them up a little. Add the figs with all the remaining ingredients and blend until you have a firm but pliable paste. You may need to add a little more water.
3 Roll the mixture into balls about the size of a cherry tomato, then roll in extra desiccated coconut to coat.
4 Store in an airtight container in the refrigerator for up to a week.

CHOCOLATE BEETROOT FUDGE CAKE
WITH PINK COCONUT CREAM & CANDIED BEETROOT SLICES

A rich fudgy special-occasion cake smothered in pink coconut cream and decorated with jewel-like candied beetroot, this makes an amazing centrepiece and is another creative contribution from the talented Wayne Glass, one of our pastry team.

This recipe is for a two-tiered cake, but if you would rather make a tray (sheet) cake, bake the full batch of cake mixture in a 28cm (11-inch) square baking tin or equivalent-sized round or rectangular baking tin. To make a 23cm (9-inch) round cake, reduce the quantities by one-third. The recipe works equally well whether you use gluten-free self-raising flour or regular wheat self-raising flour.

1   Preheat the oven to 180°C (350°F), Gas Mark 4. Line one 23cm (9-inch) and one 13cm (5-inch) cake tin with baking parchment.

2   Mix all the dry ingredients in a stand mixer fitted with the paddle attachment for 5-10 minutes until the sugar is broken up, or put in a large bowl and whisk with a balloon whisk.

3   Divide the quantity of beetroot in half. Grate one-half of the beetroot on the large-holed side of a box grater. Set aside with the orange zest and chocolate chips.

4   Measure out the wet ingredients into a blender and slice in the remaining beetroot. Blend until smooth.

5   In a large bowl, mix the dry mixture with the grated beetroot, orange zest and chocolate chips, then fold in the blended mixture.

6   Pour two-thirds of the cake mixture into the lined 23cm (9-inch) baking tin and the remaining one-third into the lined 13cm (5-inch) baking tin. Put both cakes in the oven and bake the larger one for 1 hour 20 minutes or until risen in the centre. The smaller cake will take slightly less time to cook, so check after an hour.

7   Remove each cake from the oven when done and leave to cool for a few minutes in the tin before turning out on to a wire rack to cool completely.

8   To make the candied beetroot, put the measured water and sugar in a saucepan and bring to the boil, stirring, then simmer until the sugar has dissolved.

>>

MAKES 1 × 23CM (9-INCH) AND 1 × 13CM (5-INCH) CAKE; SERVES 20-30

400g (14oz) gluten-free self-raising flour

400g (14oz) dark muscovado sugar

200g (7oz) vegan cocoa powder

4 teaspoons gluten-free baking powder

pinch of salt

400g (14oz) cooked and peeled beetroot (you can use shop-bought vacuum-packed cooked beetroot)

grated zest and juice of 2 oranges

200g (7oz) vegan dark chocolate chips (minimum 70% cocoa solids)

480ml (17fl oz) soya yogurt

350ml (12fl oz) soya milk

210ml (7½fl oz) rapeseed oil

4 teaspoons good-quality vanilla extract

FOR THE CANDIED BEETROOT SLICES

200ml (7fl oz) water

150g (5½oz) caster sugar

2 washed and peeled beetroots (if possible, use a couple of different colours of beetroot)

9   Meanwhile, slice the beetroot into very thin rounds on a mandolin or with a sharp knife. Add the beetroot slices to the sugar water and boil for about 30 minutes until they are translucent. While the beetroot slices are boiling, preheat the oven to 160°C (325°F), Gas Mark 3. Line a baking sheet with baking parchment.

10   Drain the beetroot slices from the syrup, reserving the syrup for the coconut cream, and separate out on the lined baking sheet. Bake for 1½–2 hours. To check if the beetroot slices are ready, remove one from the sheet and leave to cool for a minute. It should turn hard and brittle. Once they are ready, remove from the oven and leave to cool on the baking sheet.

11   To make the coconut cream, open the cans of coconut milk and scoop off the thick cream from the top of each into the bowl of a stand mixer fitted with the whisk attachment. (Save the watery milk for another use - *see* introduction, opposite.) Sift the icing sugar into the bowl and add the reserved beetroot sugar syrup (or beetroot juice) and vanilla, if using, then whisk following the instructions for the Coconut Whipped Cream (*see* opposite).

12   To assemble, cut each cake in half horizontally and then sandwich together with a little of the coconut cream. Spread the remaining coconut cream over the top and sides of each cake. To stack, you will need to insert 4 cake dowels or wooden skewers into the bottom tier, spaced in a circle in the centre to fit within the top tier. Sit the bottom tier on a cake board and push one dowel or skewer into the cake right down to the base. Make a mark on it at the surface of the cake, then trim all 4 dowels/skewers to the same length. Insert into the cake to come level with the surface, then sit the smaller tier securely on top.

13   Decorate the top of the cake and the ridge between the first and second tiers with the candied beetroot slices before serving.

FOR THE COCONUT CREAM
4 × 400ml (14fl oz) cans full-fat coconut milk, chilled in the refrigerator preferably overnight or at least for a few hours
200g (7oz) icing sugar
50ml (2fl oz) reserved beetroot sugar syrup from the candied beetroot (or use 3 tablespoons beetroot juice – *see* page 227 – and increase the quantity of icing sugar to 300g/10½oz)
pinch of vanilla seeds or splash of good-quality vanilla extract (optional)

COCONUT WHIPPED CREAM

SERVES 4

400ml (14fl oz) can full-fat
   coconut milk or 2 × 160ml
   (5½fl oz) cans coconut cream,
   chilled in the refrigerator
   preferably overnight or at
   least for a few hours
50g (1¾oz) icing sugar
pinch of vanilla seeds
   (optional)

Coconut whipped cream is a lovely replacement for dairy whipped cream, with the coconut flavour being surprisingly mild, and it can be flavoured variously with fruit purées, spices and syrups. You will need the thick cream from the top of a chilled can of full-fat coconut milk. Alternatively, you can use canned coconut cream, not to be confused with creamed coconut, which comes in a thick block, or cream of coconut, which is a sweet syrup. Yes, coconut is a minefield!

We've made thousands of batches of this cream, so a quick word on the method. There are loads of alarming recipes insisting that if you get one drop of the coconut water in the cream it won't work, or that you must put the mixer bowl in the freezer to chill and so on. But the method is actually much more straightforward than these would have you believe. Try to scoop off mostly the thick coconut cream from the can, but if you happen to include a little of the coconut liquid, you'll just have to whisk it longer. We've whisked this for 15 minutes or so before and it always comes together eventually.

Save the watery coconut milk for adding to a curry or soup, or for using to make Avocado Lime Cream (*see* page 123) or in smoothies. It freezes well in a zip-seal bag.

1   Open the can of coconut milk and scoop off the thick cream from the top (usually around 200g/7oz) into the bowl of a stand mixer fitted with the whisk attachment. Do the same if using creamed coconut, although there will be less liquid.

2   Sift the icing sugar into the bowl and add the vanilla, if using, then whisk on a fairly high speed until the mixture comes together, being careful not to overwhip.

VEGAN CRÈME ANGLAISE

In the great debate over whether custard or crème Anglaise should be served warm or cold, we have agreed to disagree. While Sarah is in the warm camp, though not as vehemently as one of our pastry chefs, Susie, who referred to cold custard on crumble as a "bloody travesty", Daniel thinks it's weird to have a warm custard on a warm pudding. We'll let history decide.

We use soya milk and soya cream for our crème Anglaise, but you can substitute other plant-based milks and cream, for example oat or almond. For a Christmassy flavour, you can add grated nutmeg and ground cinnamon.

1   Put all the ingredients, except the cornflour, in a medium-sized saucepan and bring to just below boiling point, stirring frequently (it will catch on the base of the pan if you don't).
2   Mix the cornflour with enough cold water to make a smooth paste, then stir into the soya milk mixture and cook for a few minutes, whisking with a balloon whisk, until thickened and glossy.
3   Strain through a sieve into a bowl and leave to cool slightly. When it cools a little, the surface may look slightly lumpy, so just whisk it again and it will become smooth.
4   Serve warm or cold, depending on your preference.

SERVES 6–8

400ml (14fl oz) soya milk
250ml (9fl oz) soya cream
150g (5½oz) caster sugar
pinch of vanilla seeds or
    1 teaspoon good-quality
    vanilla extract
25g (1oz) cornflour

SALTED CARAMEL & ESPRESSO SAUCE

SERVES 6-8

100g (3½oz) caster sugar
about 75ml (5 tablespoons)
  water
400ml (14fl oz) can full-fat
  coconut milk, chilled in the
  refrigerator preferably
  overnight or at least for
  a few hours
2 tablespoons freshly brewed
  espresso, cooled
pinch of vanilla powder
pinch of ground coffee
1 teaspoon sea salt flakes

Serve this warm over a bowl of vegan ice cream or, better yet, over a vegan sundae with maple pecans and slices of banana. A lovely way to round off a meal without too much effort.

1   To make the caramel, put the sugar in a saucepan and add the measured water - just enough to make all the sugar wet. Bring to the boil, without stirring, and simmer until the sugar starts to catch, that is when dark caramel spots begin to appear. (This takes 5-10 minutes, but don't be tempted to leave the room because you might come back to a pan full of smoking black tar.) Once the sugar has reached this stage, give the pan a quick swirl.

2   While the sugar is cooking, open the can of coconut milk and scoop off the thick cream from the top into a bowl (save the watery milk for another use - *see* introduction, page 237).

3   When the caramel has reached an even orange brown (caramel) colour, take the pan off the heat, add the espresso and whisk with a balloon whisk until it stops bubbling. Return to the heat and cook out any sugary lumps, then add the coconut cream and whisk vigorously until smooth. Reduce the heat, add the vanilla powder, ground coffee and salt and whisk for another couple of minutes.

4   Leave to cool slightly and serve warm.

5   Store the sauce in a clean airtight container in the refrigerator for up to 1 week. Reheat gently in a saucepan or in the microwave before serving.

BASICS

ALMOND FETA

The texture of the almonds here comes really close to that of crumbly feta cheese. A lot of vegan cheese recipes involve the use of a dehydrator, a bit of kit that few people can be expected to own, whereas this recipe just requires a blender and an oven.

You can eat this ridiculously convincing feta (*see* photograph overleaf) drizzled with olive oil, but we prefer to use it as a component of other dishes such as in a filling for our Pistachio and Almond Feta Kibbeh (*see* pages 44–5) or with Ezme Salad (*see* page 162).

1   Preheat the oven to 180°C (350°F), Gas Mark 4. Line a baking tray with baking parchment and brush with a little olive oil to prevent the mixture from sticking.
2   Drain the almonds, put in a blender with all the remaining ingredients and blend until smooth.
3   Turn the contents of the blender out on to the prepared tray and shape into a rough circle or square about 2.5cm (1 inch) deep.
4   Bake for 30–40 minutes until a crust has formed over the surface.
5   Leave to cool before using. Store in an airtight container in the refrigerator for up to a week.

MAKES 8–10 SERVINGS

200g (7oz) flaked almonds, soaked overnight in cold water or for a few hours in hot water

2 large garlic cloves, peeled

2 teaspoons sea salt flakes

½ tablespoon rosemary leaves

pinch of ground cumin (optional)

pinch of sumac (optional)

200ml (7fl oz) water

75ml (5 tablespoons) lemon juice

3 tablespoons extra virgin olive oil, plus extra for oiling

ALMOND CHIHUAHUA

MAKES 8-10 SERVINGS

200g (7oz) flaked almonds,
soaked overnight in cold
water or for a few hours in
hot water

2 large garlic cloves, peeled

2 teaspoons sea salt flakes

3 sprigs of oregano, leaves
picked

pinch of ground cumin

pinch of Arbol chilli flakes

pinch of ground coriander

200ml (7fl oz) water

50ml (2fl oz) lemon juice

3 tablespoons extra virgin olive
oil, plus extra for oiling

2 tablespoons lime juice

Chihuahua cheese – what a fabulous name! We fell in love with the idea of putting this best-known Mexican cheese, which is similar in taste and texture to feta, on the menu, but couldn't find any way of sourcing it, as it doesn't travel well. So we thought we would come up with our own vegan version (*see* photograph overleaf). This recipe is based on the Almond Feta (*see* opposite), but with a Mexican twist to the spices and herbs. It makes a welcome addition to many Latin American dishes – we use it in the quinoa salad featured in the Puebla Bowl (*see* pages 122-5). It can also be used as a topping for our Brazilian Black Bean Soup (*see* page 70) or to make vegan nachos.

1   Follow the instructions for Almond Feta (*see* opposite) to prepare, bake and store the "cheese".

SOYA LABNEH

Labneh (*see* photograph on previous page) is a delicious Middle Eastern cheese that is very simple to make. We find that using soya yogurt gives you a very similar creamy result to using dairy yogurt. Consequently, we have replaced our dairy version with this vegan one across our menu. We even received a complaint from someone who refused to believe this was vegan!

We often use our labneh in dips or add a smear of it with a salad, but it can be served in its own right, drizzled with olive oil and maybe sprinkled with sumac, paprika or dukkah (*see* page 196 for homemade) and scooped up with warm flatbread.

1   Mix all the ingredients together in a bowl, cover with clingfilm and leave in the refrigerator for 3–4 hours – don't skip this step, or the mixture will be too loose to hang.

2   Line a large sieve with a piece of muslin and set it over a bowl. Scoop all the mixture into the centre of the muslin. Gather up the edges of the muslin around the mixture to form a pouch and tie together with kitchen string. Tie the loose ends of the muslin around the handle of a wooden spoon. Suspend the spoon over a container deep enough to allow at least 10cm (4 inches) between the bottom of the pouch and the base of the container so that the muslin will remain clear of the liquid released by the yogurt (*see* photograph on page 241).

3   Transfer to the refrigerator and leave to drain for 12–24 hours, depending on whether you want a soft, creamy result or a firmer cheese. It will keep in the refrigerator for 5–7 days.

MAKES ABOUT 400G (14OZ)

500ml (18fl oz) soya yogurt
80ml (2¾fl oz) soya cream
1 teaspoon salt
1½ garlic cloves, very finely chopped
finely grated zest of 1 lemon

COCONUT BUTTER

**MAKES ABOUT 500G
(1LB 2OZ)**

200ml (7fl oz) soya milk
(or other plant-based milk)
1 tablespoon coconut vinegar
(or 2 teaspoons cider vinegar)
250g (9oz) coconut oil, melted
and cooled to room
temperature
2 tablespoons light oil (such
as rapeseed or sunflower)
1 teaspoon xanthan gum
pinch of salt

One of our pastry chefs, Susie Moses, introduced us to this method of making vegan butter. We've had mixed results using vegan margarines over the years, as they often give a soft finish, which is fine in some recipes but not great for crumble, pastry or shortbread where you're looking for a bit of crunch. Susie is amazing with pastry, so we asked her to improve ours and she came up with this butter. It's been a game changer.

The butter will store very well in the refrigerator for up to a month. We use a good-quality soya milk (the Bonsoy brand is the best for this), but it will also work with oat and nut milks. It's essential that the melted coconut oil is at room temperature rather than any hotter, otherwise the mixture will split.

Coconut vinegar is made from coconut water and can be sourced from health and whole food stores or online suppliers.

1   Line a plastic food container with baking parchment and place in the refrigerator.
2   Measure out the milk into a glass measuring jug and stir in the vinegar so that it curdles. Set aside.
3   Put the melted cooled coconut oil and light oil in a food processor or blender and run at a medium speed for 2–3 minutes. Then add the xanthan gum and salt and process briefly to mix.
4   With the motor running, pour in the curdled milk in a slow, steady stream and blend for 1 minute.
5   Pour the mixture into the prepared container and chill in the refrigerator or in the freezer until completely solid before using.
6   Store in the refrigerator for 2–3 weeks, or in the freezer longer term.

CASHEW CREAM

Cashew nuts blended to a paste have a particularly smooth texture similar to tahini but with a much milder flavour, and as such it's a really useful ingredient in vegan cooking. It can be used as a dressing – we serve it with our Yellow Courgette, Asparagus and Pea Shoot Salad (*see* page 62) and for topping a pide with artichokes and rocket (*see* page 108) – or as a substitute for soured cream/yogurt, to top burritos for example, or as a lovely creamy dip.

We use a touch of achiote paste in this recipe, which is made from the seeds of the achiote tree and is a key ingredient in Mexican cooking, especially pibil marinades. It imparts a fantastic orange/yellow colour and a pleasant sour flavour similar to lemon juice or tamarind. It is readily available online, but if you can't get it you can simply omit it, replicating the colour by adding a very small pinch of turmeric and introducing a little sour flavour with a pinch of sumac.

1   Drain the cashew nuts, put in a blender with all the remaining ingredients and blend until completely smooth. You can add more water if you prefer a thinner texture.

2   Store in a clean airtight jar or other container in the refrigerator. It will keep for up to a week.

MAKES 8–10 SERVINGS

200g (7oz) cashew nuts, soaked overnight in cold water or for a few hours in hot water

10g (¼oz) nutritional yeast flakes

pinch of ground cumin

pinch of chilli flakes

½ teaspoon garlic powder

pinch of achiote paste

½ tablespoon sea salt flakes

about 100ml (3½fl oz) water

SAUSAGE & BURGER BASE MIX

MAKES 500G (1LB 2OZ)

400g (14oz) stale white bread
   or sourdough bread, cut into
   small cubes
½ teaspoon salt
100g (3½oz) vegetarian suet

This simple mixture is the secret to perfect-textured veggie sausages and burgers (*see* our Smoked Tofu and White Bean Sausages, page 81). We have specially developed this formula to bind the vegetables and pulses together and add texture without imparting any unwanted additional flavours.

1   Preheat the oven to 180°C (350°F), Gas Mark 4.
2   Spread the bread cubes out on a baking sheet, sprinkle with the salt and bake for 25–30 minutes until the bread has dried out completely and is crispy.
3   Remove from the oven and leave to cool.
4   Mix with the suet until well combined, then store in an airtight container in a cool, dry place for 2–3 weeks.

WHITE WINE GRAVY

This is a nice light gravy, perfect for serving with our Butternut Squash and Tofu Terrine (*see* pages 100-1).

To make a red wine version of the gravy, simply use the same proportions of red wine and the Dark Vegetable Stock (*see* opposite) instead of the light stock.

1   Pour the white wine into a saucepan and boil until reduced to just a couple of tablespoons.
2   Add all the remaining ingredients, except the cornflour, and bring to the boil. Boil for 10 minutes.
3   Mix the cornflour with enough cold water to make a smooth paste, then stir into the pan and simmer for 2-3 minutes, stirring, until thickened. If any lumps have formed, strain the gravy through a sieve to remove before serving.

SERVES 6-8

75cl bottle dry white wine
1 litre (1¾ pints) Light
   Vegetable Stock
   (*see* opposite)
2 tablespoons tamari
1 tablespoon demerara sugar
3 tablespoons tomato ketchup
1½ tablespoons cornflour

CIDER JUS

We use this autumnal gravy to accompany our homemade Smoked Tofu and White Bean Sausages (*see* page 81) and Creamy Mustard Mash (*see* page 164).

1   Heat the oil in a small saucepan, add the onion and fry over a medium heat for about 15-20 minutes until it begins to caramelize and turn dark brown, stirring frequently so that it doesn't catch on the base of the pan. Reduce the heat slightly as you begin to reach the desired colour, add the garlic, thyme, rosemary and sugar and cook, stirring, for a further 1-2 minutes.
2   Add the cider, stirring to deglaze the pan, and bring to a simmer, then cook for 8-10 minutes until it has reduced by half.
3   Stir in the stock along with the apple juice and mustard, and season to taste with salt and pepper. Cook for a further 12-15 minutes, stirring occasionally, then check for seasoning.
4   If you want to thicken the jus slightly, mix the cornflour with enough cold water to make a smooth paste, stir into the jus and simmer for a couple of minutes, stirring, until thickened.

SERVES 6-8

splash of vegetable oil
1 large white onion, sliced
1 garlic clove, thinly sliced
2 sprigs of thyme, leaves picked
1 small sprig of rosemary,
   leaves picked
½ tablespoon sugar
500ml (18fl oz) cider
500ml (18fl oz) Dark Vegetable
   Stock (*see* opposite) or
   500ml (18fl oz) boiling water
   with 1 French onion stock
   cube dissolved in it
100ml (3½fl oz) apple juice
1 teaspoon Dijon mustard
1 teaspoon cornflour (optional)
salt and pepper

**MAKES 1.2–1.5 LITRES
(2–2¾ PINTS)**

DARK VEGETABLE STOCK

2 carrots, peeled

1 white onion with skin on

1 parsnip, peeled

1 fennel bulb

½ sweet potato, peeled, or
    ¼ butternut squash, peeled
    and deseeded

4 fresh shiitake mushrooms (or
    dried if you can't get fresh)

2 celery sticks

splash of olive oil

6 garlic cloves, peeled

2 sprigs each of rosemary,
    thyme and sage

2–3 bay leaves

50ml (2fl oz) Henderson's
    Relish (see page 28)

2 tablespoons tomato ketchup
    or tomato purée

3 litres (5¼ pints) water

salt

LIGHT VEGETABLE STOCK

2 large white onions, peeled

3 carrots, peeled

1 parsnip, peeled

2 fennel bulbs

4 celery sticks

splash of olive oil

6 garlic cloves, peeled

½ dessert apple (left whole)

2 sprigs each of sage, flat leaf
    parsley and dill

2–3 bay leaves

3 litres (5¼ pints) water

salt

VEGETABLE STOCK

As handy as a stock cube is, it bears no comparison to a real homemade stock, which will invariably up your cooking game flavour wise. It's also a great way of putting to good use any odds and ends that have lingered too long in the refrigerator along with vegetable trimmings.

DARK VEGETABLE STOCK

1 Roughly chop all the vegetables.

2 Heat the olive oil in a large saucepan, add the vegetables and garlic cloves and sauté over a medium heat for about 15 minutes, stirring frequently, until very darkly caramelized (close to burned).

3 Add all the remaining ingredients, bring to a simmer and cook, stirring occasionally, until the liquid has reduced by half.

4 Leave to cool a little and then strain through a fine sieve.

5 To store, leave to cool completely, then pour into an airtight plastic container and keep in the refrigerator for up to 4 days, or pour into ice-cube trays or zip-seal freezer bags and store in the freezer.

LIGHT VEGETABLE STOCK

1 Roughly chop all the vegetables.

2 Heat the olive oil in a large saucepan, add the onions and garlic cloves and gently sauté for a few minutes, stirring frequently, until the onions are starting to turn translucent.

3 Add the remaining vegetables and apple and sauté for a couple of minutes, stirring.

4 Add the rest of the ingredients, bring to a simmer and cook until the liquid has reduced by half, stirring occasionally.

5 Leave to cool a little and then strain through a fine sieve. Store as for the Dark Vegetable Stock (see above).

INDEX

GLOSSARY OF UK/US TERMS

UK	US
Apple purée	Applesauce
Aubergine	Eggplant
Baking parchment	Parchment paper
Beetroot	Beet
Bicarbonate of soda	Baking soda
Bramley apple	Use Pippin or Golden Delicious
Broad beans	Fava beans
Butter beans	Lima beans
Caster sugar	Superfine sugar
Chestnut mushrooms	Cremini mushrooms
Chinese cabbage	Napa cabbage
Cider vinegar	Apple cider vinegar
Clingfilm	Plastic wrap
Coriander	Cilantro
Cornflour	Cornstarch
Courgette	Zucchini
Dark chocolate	Semisweet chocolate
Dessicated coconut	Dry unsweetened coconut
Double cream	Heavy cream
Fairy cake cases	Cupcake liners
Fast-action dried yeast	Active dry yeast
Flaked almonds	Slivered almonds
Full-fat	Whole
Glacé cherries	Candied cherries
Gram flour	Chickpea (besan) flour
Greaseproof paper	Wax paper
Griddle pan	Ridged grill pan
Groundnut oil	Peanut oil
Gyoza wrapper	Can substitute with spring roll rice paper wrapper
Hob	Stove
Icing sugar	Confectioners' sugar
Kitchen paper	Paper towels
Larder	Pantry
Maris Piper potatoes	Use Yukon Gold potatoes

UK	US
Measuring jug	Liquid measuring cup
Mince	Ground, ground meat
Muffin cases	Muffin liners
Mung dahl	Yellow lentils
Muslin	Cheesecloth
Mustard powder	Dry mustard
Pak choi	Bok choy
Passata	Tomato puree
Petit pois	Baby garden peas
Piping bag	Pastry bag
Plain flour	All-purpose flour
Polenta	Italian medium to coarse cornmeal (grits)
Porridge oats	Rolled oats
Pudding bowl	Dome-shape ovenproof bowl
Rapeseed oil	Canola oil
Rocket	Arugula
Self-raising flour	Use all-purpose flour and add 1 teaspoon baking powder per 125g (4½oz) of flour
Sieve	Strainer
Single cream	Light cream
Spring greens	Collard greens
Spring onion	Scallion
Starter	Appetizer
Stock cube/powder	Bouillon cube/powder
Stoned	Pitted
Strong white flour	White bread flour
Sultanas	Golden raisins
Sun-blushed tomatoes	Semi-dried tomatoes
Tea towel	Dish towel
Tenderstem broccoli	Broccolini
Tomato purée	Tomato paste
Vegetarian suet	Solid vegetable shortening
White cabbage	Green cabbage

ACKNOWLEDGEMENTS

The Mildreds team would like to thank everyone who has been involved in making this an absolute corker of a cookbook. And a special thank you to Nico, Sylvia and Anna.